Perfect Borders, Corners & Frames for Scrapbooks

*Techniques, Templates, and Design Ideas
for Creating Beautiful Pages*

QUARRY

First published in the United States of America by:
Quarry Books, an imprint of
Rockport Publishers, Inc.
33 Commercial Street
Gloucester, Massachusetts 01930-5089
Telephone: (978) 282-9590
Fax: (978) 283-2742

www.rockpub.com

Library of Congress Cataloging-in-Publication data available

ISBN 1-59253-119-9

10 9 8 7 6 5 4 3 2 1

Layout: *tabula rasa* graphic design
Photography: Kevin Dilley/Klik Photo
Illustrations: Cherie Hanson

Printed in Singapore

Perfect Borders, Corners & Frames for Scrapbooks

Techniques, Templates, and Design Ideas for Creating Beautiful Pages

GLOUCESTER MASSACHUSETTS

QUARRY BOOKS

Trice Boerens

Contents

Introduction

The building blocks of scrapping have long consisted of three things—decorative borders, frames, and corners. In the past, albums were merely books for photo storage. They were nothing more than two-dimensional archives. Fairly recently, however, decoration was added to the pages and the rest is scrapbooking history. Albums went from monochrome to monumental.

These decorations have become more complex and florid, but a good page is still a good page—one that most often consists of a great photo accented by a border, frame, or corner.

This book contains fourteen two-page layouts of borders, ten two-page layouts of frames (each with instructions for two or more frames), and six two-page layouts of corners. As a wrap-up, the last chapter features combinations of the three. While working from this book, you may re-create the pages by imitating the photos, or you may pick and chose individual projects to mix with your own favorite themes or techniques.

The included projects were designed with the visual elements weighted to the outside of the pages—we anticipated that you will most likely be inserting the pages into albums where the inside edges of the pages are obscured by the binding. In addition, care has been taken to keep the decorative elements secondary. Your photos should always be enhanced by the decorative embellishments and never overpowered by clutter.

General Instructions

Many adhesives are available for use with this craft, and it is important to use glue that will not discolor the paper or cause it to disintegrate with age. Be sure to use products that are labeled as archival quality to prevent future damage to the paper or photos.

Most of the projects in this book call for both adhesive spray and double-sided adhesive sheets. Some applications require one or the other. Intricate shapes or uneven areas are best coated with adhesive spray, as it is too time-consuming to cut enough pieces of the double-sided adhesive to keep all the edges secure. However, when a material, such as plastic or balsa wood, requires more grip, double-sided adhesive works best.

In addition, most of the projects in this book require a metal-edged ruler and a craft knife. These tools are used to trim the photos, to cut outside edges and windows of frames, and to cut any other straight lines. Use a self-healing cutting mat to cut on, and hold the ruler firmly as a guide for the blade. Take care to change the blade in your craft knife often. Paper quickly dulls metal blades, and dull blades will make your paper edges ragged.

All measurements are listed as width x height.

Spring Break

Multimedia layered border

Layering is what makes this project interesting. With the vellum on the paper, the tissue on the vellum, the netting on the tissue, and the trim on the netting, you can build an aquatic scene worthy of your favorite vacation photos.

Instructions for the Water Borders

1. Coat the back of the vellum sheet with spray adhesive. Place the vellum on the white paper and press to adhere.

2. From the turquoise and lavender tissue paper, cut several 2" x 13" (5.1 cm x 33 cm) lengths. Trim two strips to create one wavy edge, leaving the remaining edge straight. Trim both sides of remaining lengths to make wavy strips. Coat the backs of the strips with spray adhesive. Press the narrow strips in place on the sides of the pages, overlapping where desired. Matching the straight edges of the wide strips with the sides of the pages, press in place. Trim the edges of the tissue.

3. From the netting, cut one 5" x 12" (12.7 cm x 30.5 cm) rectangle. Coat the back of the netting with spray adhesive. Place the netting on the right side of the right-hand page and press to adhere.

4. From the pastel trim, cut three lengths, 3" (7.6 cm), 4" (10.2 cm), and 7" (17.8 cm). Referring to the photo for placement, machine stitch the trim to the right-hand page.

Instructions for Completing the Pages

1. Trim the photos.

2. Use the adhesive sheet to mount the selected photos on the tan and mint papers. Trim the colored papers to make narrow borders.

3. Use the tracing paper to make the fish template (see below). From the light turquoise paper, cut one 7" x 4" (17.8 cm x 10.2 cm) rectangle. Referring to the photo for colors, draw the desired letters on the assorted papers. Cut out the letters and fish.

4. Arrange the rectangle, photos, letters, and fish on the pages. Use adhesive to attach the components to the pages. Use the colored pencils to write captions.

MATERIALS

12" x 12"
(30.5 cm x 30.5 cm)
white paper

12" x 12"
(30.5 cm x 30.5 cm)
polka dot vellum

turquoise tissue paper

lavender tissue paper

turquoise polyester netting

pastel trim with matching sewing thread

paper in the following colors:
pink, lavender, light turquoise, dark turquoise, mint, tan, gold

spray adhesive

double-sided adhesive sheet, such as Peel-N-Stick

TOOLS

metal-edged ruler

craft knife

tracing paper

pencil

scissors

sewing machine

blue colored pencil

pink colored pencil

Fish Template

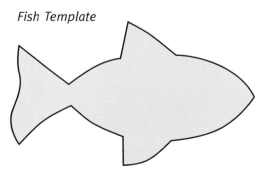

Party Umbrellas

Party favor border

It's a tropical party when you drop a paper umbrella into your glass. Combine these umbrellas and transform them from kitsch to chic by creating a beautiful abstract border. (If only you could do the same with your old grass skirt.)

Instructions for the Umbrella Border

1. Open an umbrella and, with the scissors, carefully clip the supports that connect the paper ring to the ribs of the umbrella. Run the craft knife around the top of the umbrella to remove the paper from the center toothpick. Set the iron to a medium setting and press the paper circle flat. Repeat with the remaining umbrellas.

2. Coat the backs of all but one of the paper circles with spray adhesive. Note that one circle is attached to the page with the ribs exposed, which means you'll need to spray the front of one umbrella. Overlapping as desired, place the circles along the top edges of the pages and press to adhere. Trim the overhanging edges of the circles.

Instructions for Completing the Pages

1. Trim the photos.

2. Use adhesive to mount the photos on the tan and blue papers. Trim the colored papers to make narrow borders.

3. Loop short lengths of the floss through the labels and trim the floss ends. Arrange the labels and photos on the pages. Use the double-sided adhesive to attach the components to the pages.

MATERIALS

12" x 12" (30.5 cm x 30.5 cm) brown paper

ten paper umbrellas in assorted colors (approximately 3¼" [8.2 cm] in diameter)

tan paper

blue paper

spray adhesive

double-sided adhesive sheet, such as Peel-N-Stick

gray embroidery floss

faux metal labels

TOOLS

metal-edged ruler

craft knife

scissors

iron

MATERIALS

12" x 12"
(30.5 cm x 30.5 cm)
print green paper

faux metal stickers

vintage postcard

printed
announcement

tan tissue paper

floral tissue paper

pink twine

spray adhesive

double-sided
adhesive sheet,
such as Peel-N-Stick

TOOLS

metal-edged ruler

craft knife

scissors

black fine-tip
marker

An Engaging Couple

Scalloped tissue paper border

Use floral tissue to bring up the curtain on your new life together.
Vintage papers and trendy stickers serve as the perfect accents.

Instructions for the Curtain Border

1. From the tan tissue paper, cut two 12½" x 3" (31.8 cm x 7.6 cm) strips. From the floral tissue paper, cut two 12½" x 3" (31.8 cm x 7.6 cm) strips. Referring to the diagram (see below), cut scallops along one edge of each strip.

2. Coat the backs of the floral strips with spray adhesive. With ¼" (5 mm) of the tan tissue exposed, place the floral strips on the tan strips and press to adhere. Coat the backs of the layered strips with spray adhesive. With ½" (1.3 cm) over-hanging the top edge of the pages, pinch the tissue together slightly at the scallops and press in place. Wrap the overhanging edge to the back of the pages and press to adhere.

3. From the pink twine, cut eight 5" (12.7 cm) lengths. Using the sharp point of the craft knife, pierce the paper at each scallop. Carefully thread the twine through each hole and knot. Trim the twine ends.

Instructions for Completing the Pages

1. Trim the photos.

2. Arrange the announcements, postcard, and photos on the pages. Use double-sided adhesive to attach the components to the pages. Attach the stickers to the pages. With the marker, write a messages on the stickers.

12½" (31.8 cm)

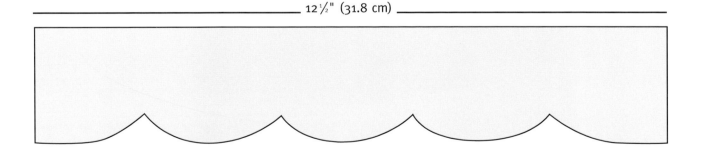

PLEASE JOIN US
FOR A WEDDING BRUNCH HONORING
DANIEL AND JENNIFER
LITTLE AMERICA HOTEL
500 S. MAIN STREET, SALT LAKE CITY
MARCH 13, 2004 AT 10:30 A.M.

MR. AND MRS. CHADRICK DALE PERKINS
REQUEST THE PLEASURE OF YOUR COMPANY
AT THE WEDDING RECEPTION OF THEIR DAUGHTER
Jennifer Lynn
AND
Daniel Joseph
SON OF MR. AND MRS. BRUCE FRED GLADWELL
ON SATURDAY, THE THIRTEENTH DAY OF MARCH
TWO THOUSAND AND FOUR

alex

Best FriendS

Piper

Best Friends

Paper pinwheel border

A border of cut and folded spinning pinwheels underlines the playful bond between a boy and his dog.

Instructions for the Pinwheels

1. From the blue print paper, cut five 2½" (6.4 cm) squares. Refer to Diagram A (see opposite, below) and, from each corner, make a 1⅛" (2.8 cm) diagonal cut. Place the squares on the work surface with the solid side facing up. Referring to Diagram B (see opposite, below), fold the bottom left corner to the center of the square. Working counterclockwise, fold the remaining corners to the center, overlapping the points.

2. Stitch a button in the center of each pinwheel, securing all layers. Tape the thread ends to the back of the pinwheels. Trim the thread ends.

3. From the dark blue paper, cut five ⅜" x 2¼" (1 cm x 5.7 cm) strips. Align the strips to the pinwheels at right angles, and tape one end of each strip to the center back of each pinwheel.

Instructions for Completing the Pages

1. From the vellum, cut one 2¾" x 8" (7 cm x 20.3 cm) rectangle. From the lavender paper, cut one 2¾" x 8" (7 cm x 20.3 cm) rectangle. With the computer printer, print the title on the white paper. Cut irregular shapes around each letter.

2. Trim the photos.

3. Arrange the rectangles, photos, and title on the pages. With the strips overhanging the bottom edges, place the pinwheels on the pages. Use adhesive to attach the components to the pages. Trim the overhanging ends of the strips. Use the marker to write captions.

MATERIALS

12" x 12" (30.5 cm x 30.5 cm) ivory paper

pink striped vellum

paper in the following colors: white, lavender, dark blue, blue print with a solid color on the reverse side

five miniature buttons

blue sewing thread

spray adhesive

double-sided adhesive sheet, such as Peel-N-Stick

TOOLS

metal-edged ruler

craft knife

sewing needle

scissors

computer printer

paper tape

black fine-tip marker

Diagram A

Diagram B

1⅛" (2.8 cm)

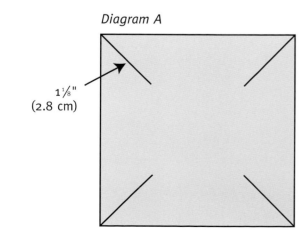

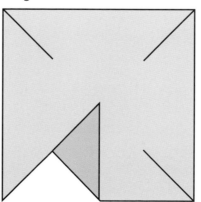

At the Park

Accented silver mesh border

This shiny mesh paper suggests the chain-link fences at a neighborhood playground. Add a little fun to the backdrop with brads and bright paper accents.

Instructions for the Playground Border

1. Cut one 13" (33 cm) length of paper mesh. Remove the protective paper from the back of the mesh and, angling it up slightly, press it in place along the top of the left-hand page. Wrap the overhanging edges to the back of the page.

2. Cut one 4½" (11.4 cm) length and one 9½" (24.1 cm) length of silver paper mesh. Attach the paper mesh strips to the top of the right-hand page, with the short strip angling up and the long strip angling down. Overlap the strip ends slightly. Wrap the overhanging edges to the back of the page.

3. From the lavender paper, cut five ¾" (1.9 cm) squares. From the brown paper, cut two ½" (1.3 cm) squares. Place the squares at random points on the paper mesh. With the sharp point of the craft knife, pierce through the centers of the squares and through the rust paper. Insert the silver brads in the holes and secure through all layers.

Instructions for Completing the Pages

1. Copy the selected photos on a copy machine. You can experiment with the copy machine settings to enhance the contrast.

2. Trim the photos and the black and white copies.

3. Arrange the photos and the black-and-white copies on the pages. Coat the backs with spray adhesive. Place on the pages and press to adhere.

4. From the red print paper, cut irregular shapes slightly larger than the letters. Arrange the pewter letters on the pages. Following the manufacturer's directions, attach the letters to the pages.

MATERIALS

12" x 12" (30.5 cm x 30.5 cm) rust colored paper

silver paper mesh with self adhesive backing

small silver brads

paper in the following colors: lavender, brown, red print

pewter tack-on letters

spray adhesive

TOOLS

metal-edged ruler

craft knife

scissors

copy machine

12" x 12"
(30.5 cm x 30.5 cm)
polka dot paper

paper in the follow-
ing colors: laven-
der, pink print,
cream print

three paper
butterflies

gray acrylic paint

spray adhesive

double-sided
adhesive sheet,
such as Peel-N-Stick

TOOLS

metal-edged ruler

craft knife

tracing paper

pencil

scissors

paintbrush

lavender colored
pencil

Paper Dolls

Accordion-style paper cut borders

Children everywhere love to make paper dolls. Weave these paper borders into your compositions to accent pages and to honor this timeless craft.

Instructions for the Paper Doll Borders

1. Use the tracing paper to make the templates (see below). From the pink print paper, cut two 2" x 4¾" (5.1 cm x 12.1 cm) strips. With the print side facing out, fold the strips accordion style with each fold measuring ¾" (1.9 cm) wide. Trace the heart template on the outside folds. Cut through the folded layers to make three connecting hearts per strip.

2. From the lavender paper, cut one 2½" x 6" (6.4 cm x 15.2 cm) strip. Fold the strip accordion style with each fold measuring 1" (2.5 cm) wide. Trace the doll template on the outside fold. Cut through the folded layers to make three connecting dolls. From the lavender paper, cut one 2½" x 4" (6.4 cm x 10.2 cm) strip. Fold and cut to make two connecting dolls.

Instructions for Completing the Pages

1. Trim the photos.

2. From the cream print paper, cut one 1" x 11" (2.5 cm x 27.9 cm) strip. Arrange the strip, photos, heart border, doll borders, and butterflies on the pages. Use adhesive to attach the components to the pages.

3. With the acrylic paint, paint the titles. Let dry. With the colored pencil, write captions.

Heart Template   *Doll Template*

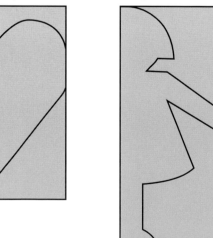

Cousins

Mary and Ivy

Sisters

Jane and

Cath and Megan

Friends

Callie and Mellissa at the
wedding

Mellissa Morgan
weds
Todd Anderson
June 8, 2004

Angels

Celestial ribbon borders

A heavenly mix of surfaces, textures, and techniques. Fashion these borders to commemorate special occasions and special relationships.

Instructions for the Angel Borders

1. Spacing evenly, stamp three angels along the left edge of the left-hand page. Let dry.

2. Punch a hole in the top left corner, 1" (2.5 cm) from the top and the left side of the page. Repeat in the bottom left corner. Thread the ribbon from the back to the front through the top hole, and from the front to the back through the bottom hole. Referring to the photo for placement, stitch four cross-stitches to secure the ribbon to the paper. Tape the thread ends to the back of the page and trim. Bring the ribbon ends from the back and thread them through the holes again. Tape the ribbon ends to the back of the page and trim.

3. Stamp a band of leaf fronds along the right edge of the right-hand page, approximately 1½" (3.8 cm) wide. Alter the direction of the stamp to create an irregular pattern. Let dry

4. From the mauve paper, cut three 2¼" (5.7 cm) squares. Stamp an angel in the center of each square. Let dry. Laminate the stamped squares. With the ruler and knife, trim the laminated squares to 2½" (6.4 cm).

5. Referring to the diagram (see below), punch holes in the top and bottom of each square. Loosely thread the ribbon through the holes. Use double-sided adhesive to attach the laminated squares to the right side of the right-hand page. Trim the ribbon ends.

Instructions for Completing the Pages

1. Trim the pink print paper to 8½" x 11" (21.6 cm x 27.9 cm). Coat the back of the paper with spray adhesive. Place the paper on the left-hand page. Press to adhere.

2. Trim the photos.

3. Use adhesive to mount the selected photo on the gray paper. Trim the gray paper to make a narrow border.

4. Arrange the photos on the pages. Use adhesive to attach the photos to the pages. Write a caption with the brown colored pencil.

MATERIALS

12" x 12" (30.5 cm x 30.5 cm) wheat paper

paper in the following colors: pink print, gray, mauve

laminating sheets

1 yard (0.9 m) of ⅝" (1.6 cm)-wide organza ribbon

cream thread

spray adhesive

double-sided adhesive sheet, such as Peel-N-Stick

tape

TOOLS

metal-edged ruler

craft knife

scissors

needle

leaf frond rubber stamp

angel rubber stamp

brown ink pad

¼" (5 mm) hole punch

brown colored pencil

Punch Diagram

1" (2.5 cm)

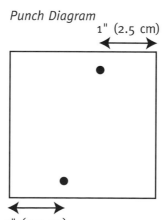

1" (2.5 cm)

HaPPy HaLLoWeen

the bear

tinkerbell

neighborhood kids

spiders
snakes
creepy
crawley
insects
bats
ravens
werewolves
spiders
snakes
creepy
crawley
insects
bats
ravens

Happy Halloween

Stung spiders Halloween border

Funny, furry spiders dangle from this whimsical Halloween border. Use it to showcase your darling kids in their scary costumes. (Or is it scary kids in darling costumes?)

Instructions for the Spider Border

1. Cut 1½" (3.8 cm)-wide strips from the corrugated paper. Cut notches along one side of the strips. Piecing as necessary, arrange the corrugated strips along the top edges of the pages. Break the strips for a diagonal photo if desired.

2. Cut five 9" (22.9 cm) lengths of pearl cotton. Wrap the lengths around the notches of the corrugated strips and knot to secure. Referring to the diagram (see below right), make small tassels for spiders. Tie the tassels to the pearl cotton at various lengths. Trim the thread ends of the spiders to shape.

Instructions for Completing the Pages

1. Trim the photos and title box. Punch a hole in the top left corner of the title box. Use the computer printer to print a message box on the purple paper. Trim the message box.

2. Arrange the photos, title box, and message box on the pages. Tie the title box to the border. Trim the thread ends.

3. Use double-sided adhesive to attach the photos, title box, message box, and border to the pages. Use the marker to write captions.

MATERIALS

12" x 12" (30.5 cm x 30.5 cm) lavender colored paper

rust colored corrugated paper

purple paper

black pearl cotton

preprinted title box

double-sided adhesive sheet, such as Peel-N-Stick

TOOLS

metal-edged ruler

craft knife

scissors

¼" (5 mm) hole punch

computer printer

black fine-tip marker

Spider Diagram

MATERIALS

12" x 12"
(30.5 cm x 30.5 cm)
green printed paper

paper in the
following colors:
light green, dark
green, orange, tan,
purple, gray, blue,
blue print

paper tape

spray adhesive

double-sided
adhesive sheet,
such as Peel-N-Stick

TOOLS

metal-edged ruler

craft knife

tracing paper

pencil

scissors

¼" (5 mm) hole
punch

black fine-tip
marker

Summer at the Lake

Rippling seaside border

The bad news—the mosquitoes are biting; the good news—so are the fish. Delight young nature lovers and old fishermen alike with this animated border.

Instructions for the Fish Border

1. Use the tracing paper to make the templates (see below). Referring to the photo for colors, cut the fish and the shadows from the assorted papers. Coat the backs of the fish with spray adhesive. Place the fish on the shadows and press in place.

2. From the gray paper, cut three ¼" x 3" (5 mm x 7.6 cm) strips. Tape the strips to the backs of the fish.

3. From the blue and blue print papers, tear several wavy strips of various lengths and widths. Overlapping where desired, arrange the waves on the bottom edges of the pages. Tuck the ends of the fish supports between the waves. Coat the backs of the waves and the fish with spray adhesive and press in place to adhere. Trim the overhanging edges of the waves.

Instructions for Completing the Pages

1. Trim the photos. From the gray paper, cut one 1" x 8" (2.5 cm x 20.3 cm) strip for the title. Punch a hole in each end of the strip.

2. Arrange the photos and title box on the pages. Use adhesive to attach the components to the pages. Use the marker to write the title and captions.

Fish Template

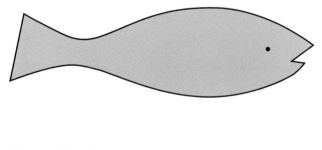

Shadow Template

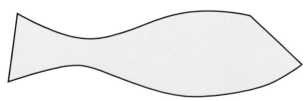

Miss Jenny's
Dance Class
Spring 2004

Sepia Dancers

Magic wand and streamer borders

Grant your favorite dancer's wish with these dreamy borders. The magic will be preserved long after the pink slippers are put away.

Instructions for the Magic Wand and Stars Border

1. Paint the dowel. Let dry. With the craft knife, cut a ½" (1.3 cm) long slit in one end of the dowel.

2. Use the tracing paper to make the star templates (see page 88). From the white paper, cut one large star. From the white vellum, cut three medium stars and two small stars. From the gold vellum, cut one medium star. From the yellow paper, cut one small star.

3. Coat the front of the large white star with spray adhesive. Sprinkle the front of the star with glitter. Slide the star into the slit at the end of the dowel to make a magic wand. Coat the fronts of three white vellum stars with spray adhesive. Sprinkle the stars with glitter.

4. From the gold vellum, cut one 1" x 12" (2.5 cm x 30.5 cm) strip. Referring to the diagram (see opposite, below), cut contours in the sides of the strip. With the craft knife, cut eleven small holes in the strip. Thread the wand through the holes. Place the wand on the work surface and crease to flatten slightly. Apply narrow strips of double-sided adhesive to the back of the creased vellum at the areas that will make contact with the page.

5. From the gold vellum, cut five narrow streamers. Curl the streamers with scissors. Place the streamers on the work surface and crease to flatten. Trim the streamers to various lengths.

6. Attach the wand to the top of the left-hand page. Arrange the streamers and the stars on the pages. Coat the backs of the stars and the streamers with spray adhesive, and press in place to adhere. Trim the overhanging stars. Use the foam spacers to attach the yellow star to the page.

Instructions for Completing the Pages

1. Trim the photos.

2. Use adhesive to mount the photos on the burgundy and olive papers. Trim the colored papers to make narrow borders.

3. Arrange the photos on the pages. Use spray adhesive for the top photos and the foam spacers for the bottom photos. Attach them to the pages. Use the marker to write a caption.

MATERIALS

12" x 12"
(30.5 cm x 30.5 cm)
pink paper

paper in the following colors:
white, burgundy, olive, pale yellow

white vellum

gold vellum

9½" (24.1 cm) long dowel or balloon stick (⅛" [3 mm] in diameter)

white acrylic paint

white glitter

spray adhesive

double-sided adhesive sheet, such as Peel-N-Stick

foam adhesive spacers

TOOLS

metal-edged ruler

craft knife

tracing paper

pencil

scissors

paintbrush

black fine-tip marker

Diagram

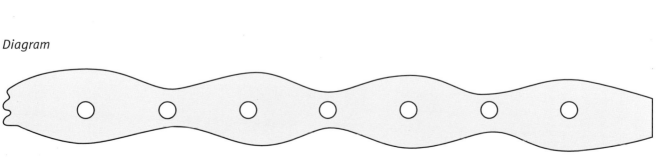

Come on OVER
for a
POOL
PARTY!!!!!!!!!!

Pool Party

Summer shapes paper and fiber border

Surf's up! Though the surfing takes place in a rubber wading pool, it's still a terrific way to cool off. Have fun making this splashy summer border.

Instructions for the Pool Party Borders

1. From the white vellum, cut two 1¼" x 12" (3.1 cm x 30.5 cm) strips. Coat the backs of the vellum strips with spray adhesive. Place the strips along the top edges of the pages and press to adhere.

2. Use the tracing paper to make the templates for the beach ball, stripes, bucket, and shovel (see page 88). Referring to the photo for colors, cut the shapes from the assorted papers. Coat the backs of the beach ball stripes with spray adhesive. Place the stripes on the balls and press to adhere.

3. With the craft knife, cut small holes in three of the beach balls. Thread three of the beach balls, two buckets, and two shovels on the light blue yarn.

4. Coat the backs of the remaining beach balls with spray adhesive. Referring to the photo for placement, press in place on the top of the left-hand page. Coat the backs of the connected shapes with spray adhesive. Press in place on the top of the right-hand page.

Instructions for Completing the Pages

1. With the computer printer, print the title on white paper. Trim the title box and photos.

2. Use adhesive to mount selected photos and the title box on the pink print paper. Trim the pink print paper to make narrow borders.

3. Punch a hole in the title box and thread a short length of dark blue yarn through the hole. Trim the yarn ends. Arrange the photos and title box on the pages. Use adhesive to attach the components to the page. Use the marker to write a caption.

MATERIALS

12" x 12" (30.5 cm x 30.5 cm) green print paper

white vellum

paper in the following colors: white, gray, light green, dark green, light blue, turquoise, mauve, pink print

light blue decorative yarn

dark blue decorative yarn

spray adhesive

double sided adhesive sheet, such as Peel-N-Stick

TOOLS

metal-edged ruler

craft knife

tracing paper

pencil

scissors

computer printer

green fine-tip marker

¼" (5 mm) hole punch

winding through-
SAN FRANCISCO

Allison riding a trolley
in San Francisco
May 28, 2004

View of the Bay

Pacific Bell Park
San Francisco Giants
verses the Atlanta Braves
May 30, 2004

Winding through San Francisco

Asian accent borders

A city teaming with activity is represented by graphic Japanese icons. Use these borders to also decorate menus or invitations.

MATERIALS

12" x 12"
(30.5 cm x 30.5 cm)
light gray paper

paper in the
following colors:
white, light gray,
medium gray,
cream, blue print

chopstick

metal medallions

gold leaf paper

rubber cement

spray adhesive

double-sided
adhesive sheet,
such as Peel-N-Stick

TOOLS

metal-edged ruler

craft knife

tracing paper

scissors

Instructions for the Kimonos and the Chopstick Border

1. From the cream paper, cut one 1½" x 12" (3.8 cm x 30.5 cm) strip. With the craft knife, cut ¾" (1.9 cm) squares at each end of the strip. Note that the space between the squares should be less than the length of the chopstick.

2. From the medium gray paper, cut two ⅜" x 3½" (1 cm x 8.9 cm) strips. Place the cream strip along the top edge of the left-hand page. Slide the gray strips behind the cream strip and center them vertically behind the windows. With the double-sided adhesive, attach the bottom ends of the strips to the page. Place the chopstick on top of the cream strip and beneath the gray strips. Fold the top ends of the gray strips to the back of the page, pulling tightly enough to secure the chopstick. With the double-sided adhesive, attach the top ends of the strips to the back of the page. Remove the chopstick.

3. Use the tracing paper to make the kimono template (see page 88). From the blue print paper, make two kimonos. From the cream paper, cut two ¼" x 4" (5 mm x 10.2 cm) strips. Fold the kimonos over the strips and center. Use the double-sided adhesive to secure the kimono layers together.

4. Cut a 1" (2.5 cm) circle in a piece of scrap paper. Center the circle on the kimonos and apply a coat of rubber cement in the exposed circle. Let dry. Place the gold leaf paper right side down on the circles and burnish. Remove any excess gold leaf.

Instructions for Completing the Pages

1. With the computer printer, print the title and captions on the white paper.

2. Trim the photos, title, and captions. Arrange the photos, kimonos, title box, and captions on the pages. Use adhesive to secure the components to the pages.

3. From the light gray paper, cut three narrow strips of varying lengths. Leaving loops large enough to insert the chopstick, thread the strips through the medallions, and secure the ends to the back of the strips with rubber cement. Thread the medallions on the chopstick and slide it under the gray strips.

12" x 12"
(30.5 cm x 30.5 cm)
ivory paper

12" x 12"
(30.5 cm x 30.5 cm)
blue print paper

paper in the
following colors:
turquoise, medium
blue, orange, dark
gray, periwinkle
with white on the
reverse side

chipboard

one large
latex balloon

turquoise curling
ribbon

spray adhesive

double-sided
adhesive sheet,
such as Peel-N-Stick

TOOLS

metal-edged ruler

craft knife

tracing paper

pencil

scissors

tape

brown colored
pencil

Birthday Balloons

Layered shapes party borders

A high-flying parade of balloons for a birthday commemoration.
The bright colors of these balloons and ribbons are the perfect
contrast to the charming sepia-toned photos.

Instructions for the Packages and Balloon Border

1. From the blue paper, cut two 2" (5.1 cm) squares. From the curling ribbon, cut four 3" (7.6 cm) lengths. Center and wrap the ribbon around the squares, both vertically and horizontally. Tape the ribbon ends to the backs of the squares with tape. From the curling ribbon, cut two 2½" (6.4 cm) lengths. Fold in half at the centers. With the ends exposed, tape the ribbon to the backs of the squares.

2. Use the tracing paper to make the template (see opposite, below). From the orange paper, cut two balloons with necks. From the periwinkle/white paper, cut two ¼" x 4" (5 mm x 10.2 cm) strips. Fold in half lengthwise and place on the bottoms of the balloons. Cut two ¼" x 2" (5 mm x 5.1 cm) strips. Wrap the strips around the necks of the balloons, overlapping the folded strips. Use double-sided adhesive to secure the ends. Trim the ends at an angle. From the turquoise, periwinkle, and orange paper, cut a total of six balloons with no necks.

3. From the chipboard, cut one balloon. Cut a slit in the back of the latex balloon and insert the chipboard balloon inside. Stretch the latex around the chipboard and trim away the excess. Secure the wrapped edges of the latex to the chipboard with several short strips of double-sided adhesive. Trim the rolled neck from the latex balloon. From the curling ribbon, cut one 13" (33 cm) length. Curl slightly and tie around the neck of the wrapped balloon.

Instructions for Completing the Pages

1. Trim the photos. Trim the blue print paper to an 11" (27.9 cm) square.

2. Arrange the blue print paper, photos, packages, and balloons on the pages. Use adhesive to attach the components to the pages. Note, attach the latex balloon with double-sided adhesive. Trim the overhanging edges of the balloons.

3. Write the title on the gray paper. Cut out the title and coat the back of the trimmed title with the spray adhesive. Press in place on the left-hand page. Use the colored pencil to complete the title.

Balloon

Ann
Liz
Joe

Greetings
From Our House
to Your House

Lisa & Maggie

BABY TELEGRAPH AND CABLE CO.
BABYGRAM

Gentler Times

Gathered paper borders

Delicate paper ruffles can float above your favorite family photos. The gathered cream paper poses as aged lace without adding bulk.

Instructions for the Gathered Paper Borders

1. From the tissue paper, cut four 2" x 20" (5.1 cm x 50.8 cm) strips. Layer two strips and machine stitch a gathering stitch along the center. Pull the bottom thread and gather evenly. Knot and trim the thread ends. Arrange the gathered strip on the page and press to flatten. Trim to the desired length. After trimming the strip, limit handling to avoid removing the gathers. Repeat with the second strip.

2. Attach the stickers to the left-hand page. Arrange one strip on the stickered page and carefully trim the tissue to frame any selected stickers.

3. Coat the back of the gathered strip with spray adhesive. Place the strip on the page and press to adhere. Arrange and attach the second strip on the right-hand page.

4. Place the beads on the right-hand page, repeating the curve of the tissue strip. With the needle, pierce the paper for bead placement. Stitch the beads to the paper and secure the thread ends to the back of the page with the tape.

Instructions for Completing the Pages

1. Trim the photos.

2. Arrange the photos and announcement on the pages. Use adhesive to attach the components to the pages. Use foam spacers to attach the selected photo to the page.

3. To make the diagonal corner stays, cut four ¼" x 4" (5 mm x 10.2 cm) strips from the gray paper. Measure and cut parallel slits along the four sides of the photo with the craft knife. Thread the strips through the slits and secure the ends to the back of the page with tape.

MATERIALS

12" x 12" (30.5 cm x 30.5 cm) blue print paper

light gray paper

birth announcement

cream tissue paper

pink sewing thread

glass flower beads

silver bugle beads

small stickers

spray adhesive

double-sided adhesive sheet, such as Peel-N-Stick

TOOLS

metal-edged ruler

craft knife

scissors

sewing machine

needle

tape

foam adhesive spacers

black fine-tip marker

Switzerland
July 12, 2004

Happy Wanderers

Shingled paper and feathered grass frames

Two distinctive textures are represented with these frames: scarred and weathered wooden shingles and shining emerald meadows.

Instructions for the Shingle Frame

1. The frame is made for a 7½" x 5" (19.1 cm x 12.7 cm) photo. Make adjustments if your photo is a different size. From the burgundy paper, cut an 8½" x 6" (21.6 cm x 15.2 cm) rectangle. Cut a 7" x 4½" (17.8 cm x 11.4 cm) window in the center.

2. From the black paper, cut several ¾" x 8½" (1.9 cm x 21.6 cm) strips. From the gray paper, cut one ¾" x 8½" (1.9 cm x 21.6 cm) strip. Cut shallow, irregular curves on one side of each strip. Cut each strip into shingles that measure from ½" to 3" (1.3 cm to 7.6 cm) long. Apply the chalk to the edges of several of the black shingles.

3. Starting at the bottom and overlapping rows, arrange the shingles on the burgundy frame. Note that random areas of the frame are left exposed and some sections overhang the outside and inside edges of the frame. Coat the backs of the shingles with spray adhesive. Press the shingles in place on the frame. Center and tape the photo to the back of the frame.

Instructions for the Grass Frame

1. The frame is made for a 5½" x 4½" (13.4 cm x 11.4 cm) photo. Make adjustments if your photo is a different size. From the sage paper, cut a 7½" x 6½" (19.1 cm x 16.5 cm) rectangle. Cut a 5" x 4" (12.7 cm x 10.2 cm) window in the center.

2. From the fabric, cut a frame with the outside edge slightly larger and the window slightly smaller than the paper frame. Remove a few loose threads along the cut edges so it frays slightly. Place the feathers on the bottom left corner of the frame. Trim to the desired lengths. With small, even stitches, secure most of the feathers to the fabric. Weave the remaining feathers over and under through the fabric. Coat the back of the fabric with spray adhesive. Center and press the fabric on the paper frame. Tape the photo to the back of the frame in the center.

Instructions for Completing the Pages

1. Trim the remaining photo. Trim the sage paper to 8" x 10" (20.3 cm x 25.4 cm). Arrange the colored papers, framed photos, unframed photo, and butterflies on the pages. Use adhesive to secure the components to the pages. Use the marker to write a caption.

MATERIALS

12" x 12" (30.5 cm x 30.5 cm) wheat colored paper

paper in the following colors: gold, sage, burgundy, black, gray

sage textured fabric

fine peacock pin feathers

painted feather butterflies

gray decorative chalk

purple decorative chalk

spray adhesive

double-sided adhesive sheet, such as Peel-N-Stick

TOOLS

metal-edged ruler

craft knife

sage sewing thread

needle

tape

green fine-tip marker

MATERIALS

12" x 12"
(30.5 cm x 30.5 cm)
oatmeal colored
paper

paper in the follow-
ing colors: light
gray, dark gray,
cream print

one 6" x 11 ¾"
(15.2 cm x 29.8 cm)
sheet birch veneer,
¹⁄₆₄" (0.8 mm) thick

walnut wood stain

faux metal letter
disks

printed
announcement

spray adhesive

double-sided
adhesive sheet,
such as Peel-N-Stick

TOOLS

metal-edged ruler

craft knife

sewing thread

scissors

paintbrush

paper towel

tape

Winter Love Scene

Elegant wood veneer frames

Large, flat areas of rich wood grain give this frame an architectural look. Small brackets provide an effective complement while keeping with the style of clean corners and spare lines.

Instructions for the Frame

1. The frame is made for a 4¼" x 6¼" (10.8 cm x 15.8 cm) photo. Make adjustments if your photo is a different size. From the dark gray paper, cut a 5" x 7" (12.7 cm x 17.8 cm) rectangle. Cut a 3¾" x 5¾" (9.5 cm x 14.6 cm) window in the center.

2. Referring to the photo for placement, and with the ruler and knife, cut a 4¼" x 6¼" (10.8 cm x 15.8 cm) window in the veneer. It will take several passes of the knife to cut completely through the wood. Coat the veneer frame with the stain. Blot the stain from the veneer to expose the grain of the wood. Let dry. Center and tape the photo to the back of the paper frame. Center and tape the framed photo to the back of the veneer frame.

Instructions for Completing the Pages

1. Trim the photos and announcement. Use spray adhesive to mount the announce-ment on the light gray paper. Trim the gray paper to create a narrow border. Attach the mounted announcement to the cream print paper. Trim the print paper to create a 1" (2.5 cm)-wide border.

2. From the dark gray paper, cut a 1" x 5½" (2.5 cm x 13.4 cm) strip. Referring to the photo for placement, stitch the disks to the paper. Tape the thread ends to the back of the strip.

3. From the remaining veneer, cut four ¾" (1.9 cm) strips. Stain the strips. Let dry. Arrange the framed photo, unframed photos, brackets, announcement, and mes-sage strip on the pages. Use double-sided adhesive to attach the components to the pages.

Dewey Jay & Jeanette Gill
are pleased to announce
the marriage of their daughter
Jealin Joyce
to
Jeremy Scott Dickamore
Son of Gene & Karleen Dickamore
On Saturday, March 6, 2004

l
o
v
e

Pinnochio
outside of Geppetto's Toy Shoppe

Wish List

puppy

candy necklace

paper

stickers

trip to the zoo

snow cone maker

sidewalk chalk

Mary and Santa - Christmas 2003

David and Melissa - Holiday Party

Christmas Wish List

Cut and fold out paper frames

The folding sections of these easy-to-make frames open to reveal treasured photos and bring to mind the paper windows and doors of a holiday advent calendar.

Instructions for the Square Frame

1. The frame is made for a 5" (12.7 cm) square photo. Make adjustments if your photo is a different size. From the wheat paper, cut a 7½" (19.1 cm) square. Draw a 4½" (11.4 cm) square in the center.

2. Referring to Diagram A (see below), cut a diamond in the square. Cut diagonal lines from corner to corner of the marked square. Score the paper along the dotted lines. Fold the points out at the scored lines. Remove any visible pencil marks with the eraser. Use the foam spacers to attach the points to the frame sides. Center and tape the photo to the back of the frame.

Instructions for the Rectangle Frame

1. The frame is made for a 2½" x 3½" (6.4 cm x 8.9 cm) photo. Make adjustments if your photo is a different size. From the tan paper, cut a 3½" x 4½" (8.9 cm x 11.4 cm) rectangle. Draw a 2" x 3" (5.1 cm x 7.6 cm) rectangle in the center.

2. Referring to Diagram B (see below), cut diagonal lines from corner to corner of the marked rectangle. Score the paper along the dotted lines. Fold the points out at the scored lines. Remove any visible pencil marks. Trim the top and bottom points.

3. From the pink paper, cut a 2¾" x 3¾" (7 cm x 9.5 cm) rectangle. Cut a 2⅛" x 3⅛" (5.4 cm x 7.9 cm) window in the center. Fold the points of the tan frame to the center. Coat the back of the pink frame with spray adhesive. Center and press in place on the tan frame. Fold the points out and use the foam spacers to attach them to the frame sides. Center and tape the photo to the back of the frame.

Instructions for Completing the Pages

1. With the computer printer, print the title on the white paper. Trim the title box to 3½" x 6½" (8.9 cm x 16.5 cm). Cut 3½" x 6½" (8.9 cm x 16.5 cm) rectangles from the red and tan papers.

2. Arrange the framed photos, rectangles, and title box on the pages. Use double-sided adhesive to attach the components to the pages. Use craft glue to attach the snowflakes to the pages. Use colored pencil to write captions.

MATERIALS

12" x 12" (30.5 cm x 30.5 cm) cream print paper

12" x 12" (30.5 cm x 30.5 cm) tan print paper

paper in the following colors: wheat, tan, pink, white, red

five tin snowflakes

spray adhesive

double-sided adhesive sheet, such as Peel-N-Stick

foam adhesive spacers

craft glue

TOOLS

metal-edged ruler

craft knife

pencil

computer printer

brown colored pencil

kneaded rubber eraser

tape

Diagram A

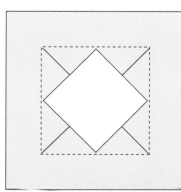

Diagram B

12" x 12"
(30.5 cm x 30.5 cm)
turquoise polka dot
paper

paper in the follow-
ing colors: white,
ivory, tan, blue,
pale green, dark
green

preprinted clock

preprinted letters

precut paper frame

foam adhesive
spacers

spray adhesive

double-sided
adhesive sheet,
such as Peel-N-Stick

TOOLS

metal-edged ruler

craft knife

tracing paper

pencil

alphabet rubber
stamps

turquoise ink pad

turquoise colored
pencil

black fine-tip
marker

tape

copy machine

Graduation Celebration

Classical column frames

After the ceremony, commence with the party. Go to the head of
the class with frames that feature classic columns as playful props.

Instructions for the Doorway Frame

1. The frame is made for a 4½" x 6¾" (11.4 cm x 17.1 cm) photo. Make adjustments
   if your photo is a different size. To achieve a gray cast, adjust the copy machine to
   the darkest setting. Make two copies of the column. Cut out the columns.

2. Use the tracing paper to make the pediment templates (see page 89). From the tan
   paper, make one large pediment. From the ivory paper, make one small pediment
   and two 2½" (6.4 cm) squares. From the pale green paper, cut one ¾" x 3⅛"
   (1.9 cm x 7.9 cm) strip.

3. Coat the backs of the small pediment, clock, and letters with spray adhesive. Center and press the small pediment on the large pediment, and then press the clock
   onto the small pediment. Press the letters on the squares. Use the colored pencil
   to shade the columns and clock.

4. Arrange the photo, columns, and green strip on the left-hand page. Use adhesive
   to attach the components to the page. Use the foam spacers to attach the pediment and the squares to the page.

Instructions for the Window Frame

1. The frame is made for a 5" x 4" (12.7 cm x 10.2 cm) photo. Make adjustments if
   your photo is a different size. Coat the back of the photo with spray adhesive and
   press on the right-hand page. Trim around the paper to make a ½" (1.3 cm) border.

2. Make four copies of the columns. Cut out the columns and shade them with the
   colored pencil. With the top ends out and overlapping at the corners, arrange the
   columns around the photo. Trim the exposed ends. Trim the ends of the bottom
   right corner at a right angle.

3. From the tan paper, cut a 1½" (3.8 cm) square. Use the tracing paper to make the
   four-leaf clover template (see page 89). From the dark green paper, cut one clover.
   Place the square at the bottom right corner. Place the clover on the square. Use
   adhesive to attach the components to the page.

Instructions for Completing the Page

1. Center and tape the small photo to the paper frame. Attach the framed photo to
   the page with double-sided adhesive. Stamp the message. Let dry. Use the marker
   to write a caption.

MATERIALS

12" x 12"
(30.5 cm x 30.5 cm)
blue polka dot
paper

12" x 12"
(30.5 cm x 30.5 cm)
gray polka dot
paper

12" x 12"
(30.5 cm x 30.5 cm)
black paper

paper in the
following colors:
light pink, light
lavender, light blue,
blue print, silver,
lavender print, pink
print with white on
the reverse side

gold embossing
powder

spray adhesive

double-sided
adhesive sheet,
such as Peel-N-Stick

TOOLS

metal-edged ruler

craft knife

scissors

rose rubber stamp

butterfly rubber
stamp

tan ink pad

black ink pad

angel clip art

tape

black fine-tip
marker

Laughing Out Loud

Glittering embossed and collaged frames

A spring day shared with an old friend and punctuated by a good laugh. Preserve a personal memory behind a sparkling, embossed, or collaged frame.

Instructions for the Embossed Frame

1. The frame is made for a 7" x 5" (17.8 cm x 12.7 cm) photo. Make adjustments if your photo is a different size. From the black paper, cut an $8\frac{3}{4}$" x $6\frac{3}{4}$" (22.2 cm x 17.1 cm) rectangle. Cut a $6\frac{1}{4}$" x $4\frac{1}{4}$" (15.8 cm x 10.8 cm) window in the center.

2. From the lavender paper, cut an $8\frac{1}{2}$" x $6\frac{1}{2}$" (21.6 cm x 16.5 cm) rectangle. Cut a $6\frac{1}{2}$" x $4\frac{1}{2}$" (16.5 cm x 11.4 cm) window in the center.

3. With the tan ink and the rose stamp, stamp a random floral pattern on the frame. Sprinkle the wet ink with embossing powder. Remove the excess powder. Apply heat with a heat gun until the powder melds to the paper. Coat the back of the frame with spray adhesive. Center and press in place on the black frame. Center and tape the photo to the back of the frame.

Instructions for the Collage Frame

1. From the blue print paper, cut a 7" x 5" (17.8 cm x 12.7 cm) rectangle. Referring to the diagram for placement, cut a $4\frac{1}{2}$" x 3" (11.4 cm x 7.6 cm) window with rounded corners.

2. From the silver paper, cut a $1\frac{1}{4}$" x 6" (3.1 cm x 15.2 cm) strip. Refer to step 2 of the Embossed Frame and emboss the floral pattern on the strip. Coat the back of the strip with spray adhesive. Press in place along the wide side of the frame.

3. From the pink print/white paper, cut two $\frac{1}{8}$" x $8\frac{1}{2}$" (3 mm x 21.6 cm) strips. Coil the strips tightly. Place the strips on the work surface and crease to flatten. Coat the backs of the strips with spray adhesive, and press in place around the edge of the frame window. Trim around the clip art. Tape the clip art to the back of the frame. From the lavender paper, cut a $5\frac{1}{2}$" x 4" (13.4 cm x 10.2 cm) rectangle. Center and tape the lavender paper to the back of the frame.

Instructions for Completing the Pages

1. From the black paper, cut a $1\frac{3}{4}$" x 12" (4.4 cm x 30.5 cm) strip, and a $2\frac{1}{2}$" x 12" (6.4 cm x 30.5 cm) strip. Coat the backs of the strips with adhesive spray. Press the narrow strip in place along the left edge of the blue page. Press the wide strip in place along the right edge of the gray page.

2. From the silver paper, cut one 2" x $1\frac{1}{2}$" (5.1 cm x 3.8 cm) rectangle. Refer to step 2 of the Embossed Frame and emboss the butterfly on the rectangle.

3. From the blue paper, cut one $6\frac{3}{4}$" x $2\frac{1}{2}$" (17.1 cm x 6.4 cm) rectangle. From the pink paper, cut one 9" x 6" (22.9 cm x 15.2 cm) rectangle. From the pink print paper, cut three $2\frac{3}{4}$" x $3\frac{1}{2}$" (7 cm x 8.9 cm) rectangles. And from the lavender print paper, cut one $2\frac{3}{4}$" x $3\frac{1}{2}$" (7 cm x 8.9 cm) rectangle.

4. Noting overlaps, arrange the trimmed papers, framed photo, and framed clip art on the pages. Use adhesive to attach the components to the pages. With the black ink, stamp the butterflies on the right-hand page. Use the marker to write a title and message.

Old Friends

We met at the park and walked
over to the restaurant inside
the old grist mill. It was
a beautiful day and was
warm enough to walk
around without coats
or sweaters. We decided
that next

Frame Diagram

1" (2.5 cm)

½" (1.3 cm)

1¾"
(4.4 cm)

1" (2.5 cm)

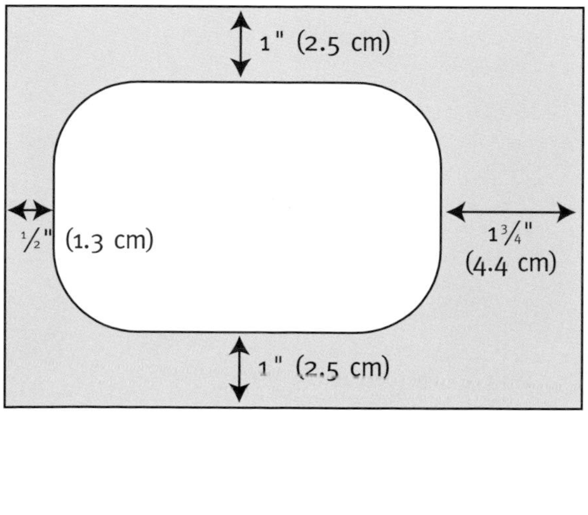

When We Were Young

Clever found-object frames

Flashback to the time of first crushes and lunch lines. Use the unique found-object decorations as your own personal time capsule.

Instructions for the Necklace Frame

1. This arrangement is made for a 4" x 6" (10.2 cm x 15.2 cm) photo. Make adjustments if your photo is a different size. From the alphabet paper, cut a 5½" x 8½" (13.4 cm x 21.6 cm) rectangle. Coat the back of the paper with spray adhesive. Referring to the photo for placement, press in place on the top of the left-hand page. Cut a 3" (7.6 cm) length of paper ribbon. Align the ribbon with the bottom right edge of the alphabet paper, and use double-sided adhesive to attach it to the page.

2. Coat the back of the photo with spray adhesive, and press in place on the page.

3. Place the necklace on the photo and smooth out the chain. Carefully lift the chain from the paper at several different points and apply a small drop of the glue at the contact point. Press the chain in place to adhere.

Instructions for the Shoelace Frame

1. This arrangement is made for a 4" x 6" (10.2 cm x 15.2 cm) photo. Make adjustments if your photo is a different size. From the alphabet paper, cut a 5½" x 8½" (13.4 cm x 21.6 cm) rectangle. Coat the back of the paper with spray adhesive. Referring to the photo for placement, press in place on the top of the right-hand page.

2. Coat the back of the photo with spray adhesive, and press in place on the page. Cut a 3" (7.6 cm) length of paper ribbon. Align the ribbon with the bottom left edge of the photo, and use double-sided adhesive to attach it to the page.

3. From the pink paper, cut a ½" x 3" (1.9 cm x 7.6 cm) strip. Use double-sided adhesive to attach the strip at a diagonal on the bottom right corner of the photo. Place the shoelace on the photo with the ends intersecting on top of the pink strip. Use short, narrow strips of double-sided adhesive to attach the shoelace to the page at three chosen contact points. Coat the back of the bubble gum label with spray adhesive and place over the lace and the pink strip, and press in place to adhere.

Instructions for Completing the Pages

1. Arrange the alphabet tiles on the ribbon.
   Attach them to the ribbon with double-sided adhesive. Arrange the remaining components on the pages. Use adhesive to attach the components to the pages.

MATERIALS

12" x 12" (30.5 cm x 30.5 cm) ivory paper

alphabet print paper

pink paper

peach paper ribbon

plastic letter tiles

one necklace

one shoelace

bubble gum label sticker

assorted items such as plastic slide frames, die-cut shapes, shirt pocket, paper tickets

spray adhesive

double-sided adhesive sheet, such as Peel-N-Stick

TOOLS

metal-edged ruler

craft knife

scissors

craft glue

MATERIALS

12" x 12"
(30.5 cm x 30.5 cm)
tan paper

paper in the follow-
ing colors: white,
black, gray, peri-
winkle

pewter star brads

yellow brads

laminating sheets

½ yard (0.5 m)
gray rayon braid

spray adhesive

double-sided
adhesive sheet,
such as Peel-N-Stick

TOOLS

metal-edged ruler

craft knife

scissors

tape

pencil

computer printer

black fine-tip
marker

Protective gallery display frames

Shine the spotlight on great art and a great artist with this sophisti-
cated presentation. The laminated surfaces protecting the artwork
and the photo resemble shiny gallery glass.

Instructions for the Lattice Frame

1. The frame is made for a 3½" x 5½" (8.9 cm x 13.4 cm) photo. Make adjustments if
   your photo is a different size. From the periwinkle paper, cut four ¼" x 9" (5 mm x
   22.9 cm) strips. With the ruler and knife, cut a 5" x 7½" (12.7 cm x 19.1 cm) rectangle
   from the laminating sheet.

2. Separate the layers of the trimmed laminating sheet. Place the dull layer on the
   work surface. Center and place the photo on top. Overhanging the corners of the
   photo slightly, arrange the strips to form a diamond. Align the clear layer of the
   laminating sheet on the dull layer and burnish.

Instructions for the Picture Frames

1. The left frame is made for 4½" x 6¼" (11.4 cm x 15.8 cm) artwork. Make adjustments if your artwork is a different size. Cut around the outside edge of the artwork.
   Laminate the artwork. With the ruler and knife, trim the laminated artwork to a
   5½" x 7¼" (13.4 cm x 18.4 cm) rectangle.

2. From the black paper, cut one 5½" x 7¼" (13.4 cm x 18.4 cm) rectangle. Cut a
   4½" x 6¼" (11.4 cm x 15.8 cm) window in the center. Using double-sided adhesive,
   attach the frame to the front of the laminated rectangle.

3. The right frame is made for 4¼" x 5¼" (10.8 cm x 13.3 cm) artwork. Making
   adjustments for the smaller size, repeat steps 1 and 2 to laminate the artwork and
   complete the frame.

Instructions for Completing the Pages

1. Referring to the photo for placement, attach the framed photo to the left-hand
   page with double-sided adhesive. From the gray paper, cut two 2¼" (6 cm)
   squares. Coat the backs of the squares with spray adhesive. Press in place beneath the strips at the top and bottom of the frame. With the sharp point of the
   craft knife, pierce through the intersecting strips and through the gray and tan
   paper. Insert the star brads in the holes and secure through all layers.

2. Cut an 8" (20.3 cm) length of rayon braid and tape the ends to the back of the
   large frame. Cut a 7" (17.8 cm) length and tape the ends to the back of the small
   frame. Place the framed pieces on the right-hand page and, with the pencil, mark
   the point at which they will "hang" from the rayon braid. Pierce the paper at the
   marked points with the craft knife. Insert the yellow brads and secure.

3. Attach small squares of double-sided adhesive to the corners on the backs of the
   frames. Loop the braid over the brads and attach them to the page. Use the computer printer to print a title and captions on the white paper. Trim the title and
   caption boxes. Use spray adhesive to attach them to the pages.

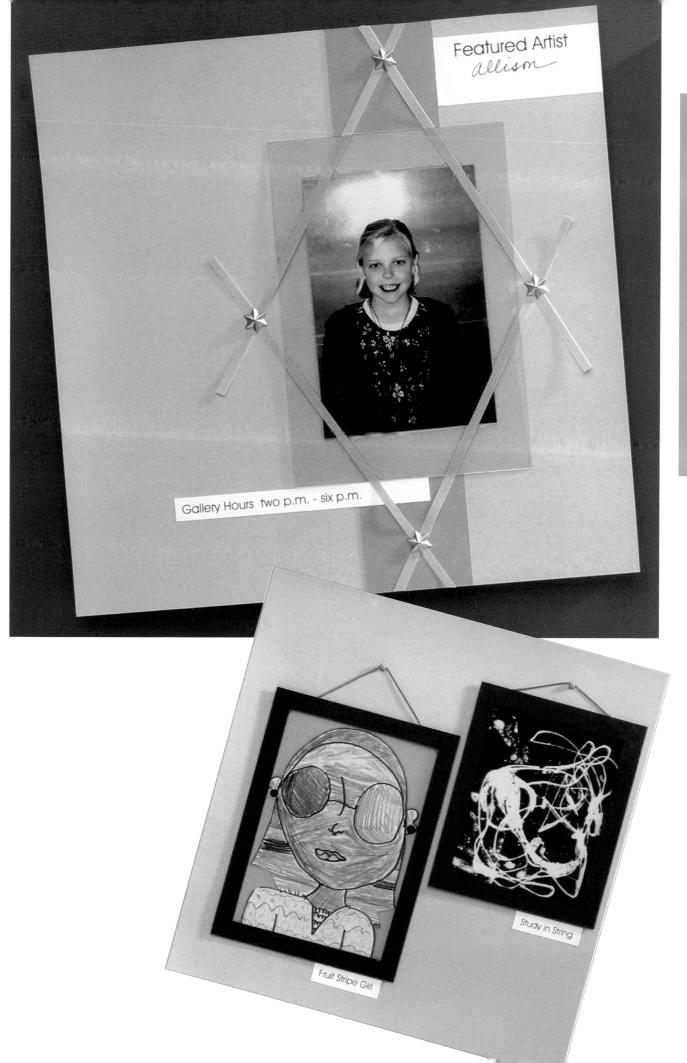

Featured Artist *allison*

Gallery Hours two p.m. - six p.m.

Fruit Stripe Girl

Study in String

MATERIALS

12" x 12"
(30.5 cm x 30.5 cm)
gray paper

12" x 12"
(30.5 cm x 30.5 cm)
script paper

12" x 12"
(30.5 cm x 30.5 cm)
taupe print paper

paper in the follow-
ing colors: black,
brown, pink/cream
patterned paper

4 mm wide purple
silk ribbon

preprinted message

preprinted accent
paper

pink vellum tag

spray adhesive

TOOLS

metal-edged ruler

craft knife

pencil

scissors

needle

tape

black fine-tip
marker

Long Ago

Heritage-style multimedia frames

A mélange of somber colors and rich textures honors the fabric of
pioneer life.

Instructions for the Herringbone Frame

1. The frame is made for a 5" x 7" (12.7 cm x 17.8 cm) photo. Make adjustments if
   your photo is a different size. From the brown paper, cut a 6¼" x 8¼" (15.8 cm x
   20.9 cm) rectangle. Cut a 4½" x 6½" (11.4 cm x 16.5 cm) window in the center.

2. Referring to Diagram A (see below), mark the dots on the left side of the frame.
   With the sharp point of the craft knife, cut small holes at the marked points. Cut a
   24" (61 cm) length of the ribbon. Place the frame right side down on the work surface. Tape the ribbon to the back of the frame ¾" (1.9 cm) above the top hole.

3. Thread one end of the ribbon through the needle. Bring the ribbon from the back
   to the front and insert the needle through the top hole. Wrap the ribbon around
   the edge of the paper, and on the front of the frame, reinsert the ribbon in the
   next hole. Continue stitching to complete one edge. Remove the needle and thread
   it on the remaining end. Repeat the stitching working in the opposite direction.
   When complete, the rows form seven V shapes. Tape the ends to the back of the
   frame. Trim the exposed ends. Center and tape the photo to the back of the frame.

Instructions for the Edged Frame

1. The frame is made for a 3½" (8.9 cm) square photo. Make adjustments if your
   photo is a different size. From the brown paper, cut a 3¾" x 4¾" (9.5 cm x 12.1 cm)
   rectangle. Referring to Diagram B (see below), mark the dots on the bottom of the
   frame. With the sharp point of the craft knife, cut small holes at the marked points.

2. Cut two 7" (17.8 cm) lengths of ribbon. Thread the needle on one length. Working
   from the back to the front, bring the needle up through the first hole. Stitch over and
   under to the opposite hole. Keep the ribbon loose while stitching. Thread the needle
   on the second length. Working from the front to the back, insert the needle through
   the same holes. Trim the ends. Coat the back of the photo with spray adhesive.
   Center and press in place leaving ⅛" (3 mm) around the top and sides of the photo.

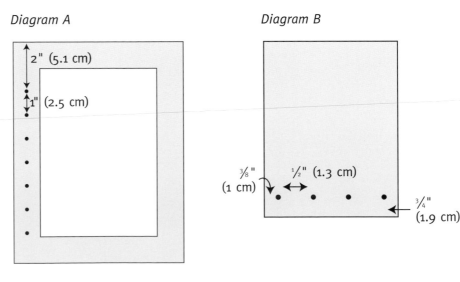

Diagram A   *Diagram B*

Instructions for Completing the Pages

1. Trim the remaining photos, message box, and paper accent. Use spray adhesive to mount the photos and message box on the brown and black paper. Trim the papers to make narrow borders.

2. Trim the script paper to 8" x 12" (20.3 cm x 30.5 cm). Trim the patterned paper to 7" x 6" (17.8 cm x 15.2 cm). Trim the taupe print paper to 3" x 12" (7.6 cm x 30.5 cm). Tear one long side of the strip. Arrange the papers, framed photo, mounted photos, and message box on the pages. Use adhesive to attach the components to the pages. Loop the tag string around the bottom V of the Herringbone Frame and knot to secure.

MATERIALS

12" x 12"
(30.5 cm x 30.5 cm)
brown paper

paper in the follow-
ing colors: gray,
black, yellow print

decorative papers

faux metal letter
disks

silver brads

fine purple wire,
24 mm

assorted beads

bronze eyelets

spray adhesive

double-sided
adhesive sheet,
such as Peel-N-Stick

TOOLS

metal-edged ruler

craft knife

wire cutters

pencil

eyelet tool

tape

computer printer

yellow colored
pencil

Families

Beaded patchwork and license plate frames

In a play, on a park bench, or at a museum—it doesn't matter where you are as long as you are together. Patchwork frames highlight family memories.

Instructions for the Beaded Frame

1. The frame is made for a $3\frac{1}{2}$" x 5" (8.9 cm x 12.7 cm) photo. Make adjustments if your photo is a different size. From the black paper, cut a $5\frac{1}{2}$" x 7" (13.4 cm x 17.8 cm) rectangle. Cut a 3" x $4\frac{1}{2}$" (7.6 cm x 11.4 cm) window in the center with the bottom of the frame slightly larger then the top and the sides.

2. From the gray paper, cut a 5" x $6\frac{1}{2}$" (12.7 cm x 16.5 cm) rectangle. Cut a $3\frac{1}{4}$" x $4\frac{3}{4}$" (8.2 cm x 12.1 cm) window in the center. Tear several strips from the decorative paper. Coat the backs of the strips with spray adhesive and place them on the gray frame in an irregular pattern. Trim the overhanging edges. Coat the back of the frame with spray adhesive. Center and press in place on the black frame.

3. Align the eyelets with the corners of the window and insert them in the black paper at the bottom of the frame. Cut an 8" (20.3 cm) length from the purple wire. Thread the beads on the wire and insert the wire ends in the eyelets. Twist the wire around itself to secure, and trim the wire ends. Center and tape the photo to the back of the frame.

Instructions for the License Plate Frame

1. The frame is made for a $5\frac{1}{2}$" x $3\frac{1}{2}$" (13.4 cm x 8.9 cm) photo. Make adjustments if your photo is a different size. From the black paper, cut a $7\frac{1}{4}$" x $5\frac{3}{4}$" (18.4 cm x 14.6 cm) rectangle. Referring to the diagram (see opposite, below), trim away the top corners of the rectangle. Cut a 5" x 3" (12.7 cm x 7.6 cm) window, with the bottom of the frame slightly larger then the top and sides.

2. From the gray paper, cut a 7" x 5" (17.8 cm x 12.7 cm) rectangle. Cut a $5\frac{1}{4}$" x $3\frac{1}{4}$" (13.3 cm x 8.2 cm) window in the center. Refer to step 2 of the Beaded Frame to apply the decorative papers. Coat the back of the frame with spray adhesive. Center and press in place on the black frame.

3. Place the disks on the frame and mark at the holes. With the sharp point of the craft knife, pierce the paper at the marked points. Insert the brads through the disks and paper and secure.

Instructions for Completing the Pages

1. Use the computer printer to print the title on the yellow paper. Trim the title box and remaining photos. Arrange the framed photos, unframed photos, and title box on the pages. Use adhesive to attach the components to the pages. Use the colored pencil to write captions.

License Plate Frame

2¼" (5.7 cm)   2¼" (5.7 cm)

½"
(1.3 cm)

½"
(1.3 cm)

SNOW DAY

Snow Day

Tulle, frost, and painted lace frames

Bundling up has never been so much fun. This bundle of three frosty frames is a perfect wintery mix, with Scribble paint used to create lacy patterns of frost and ice.

Instructions for the Tulle Frame

1. The frame is made for a 6" x 4" (15.2 cm x 10.2 cm) photo. Make adjustments if your photo is a different size. From the pink paper, cut a 7¾" x 5¾" (19.7 cm x 14.6 cm) rectangle. Cut a 5½" x 3½" (13.4 cm x 8.9 cm) window in the center. From the dark gray paper, cut a 7¾" x 5¾" (19.7 cm x 14.6 cm) rectangle. Cut a 5¾" x 3¾" (14.6 cm x 9.5 cm) window in the center. Coat the back of the gray frame with spray adhesive. Center and press in place on the pink frame.

2. Cut an 8" x 18" (20.3 cm x 45.7 cm) rectangle from the tulle and fold it lengthwise twice to 2" x 18" (5.1 cm x 45.7 cm). Tape it to the back bottom of the frame with the end extending diagonally 2" (5.1 cm) below the frame. Working from left to right, wrap the bottom of the frame several times. Tape to the back of the frame at the opposite end. From the floss, cut two 4" (10.2 cm) lengths. Wrap each around the ends of the tulle and knot to secure.

Instructions for the Painted Frost Frame

1. The frame is made for a 4" x 3¾" (10.2 cm x 9.5 cm) photo. Make adjustments if your photo is a different size. From the periwinkle paper, cut a 4½" x 4" (11.4 cm x 10.2 cm) rectangle. Cut a 3½" x 3½" (8.9 cm x 8.9 cm) window to make a frame with only three sides.

2. Squirt two or three 1" (2.5 cm) lines of paint on the frame. Blot with wax paper to cover the paper and to create a crackle pattern. Let dry. Tape the photo to the back of the frame.

Instructions for the Painted Lace Frame

1. The frame is made for a 4" x 6" (10.2 cm x 15.2 cm) photo. Make adjustments if your photo is a different size. From the polka dot paper, cut a 5½" x 7½" (13.4 cm x 19.1 cm) rectangle. Cut a 3½" x 5½" (8.9 cm x 13.4 cm) window in the center. From the light gray paper, cut a 6¼" x 8¼" (15.8 cm x 20.9 cm) rectangle. Cut a 4¼" x 6¼" (10.8 cm x 15.8 cm) window in the center. Trim to make diagonal corners 1¾" (4.4 cm) in from each corner.

2. Apply the paint in irregular swirls on the gray frame. Let dry. Coat the back of the gray frame with spray adhesive. Center and press in place on the polka dot frame. Center and tape the photo to the back of the frame.

Instructions for Completing the Pages

1. Use the computer printer to print the title on the lavender paper. Trim the title box.

2. From the gray paper, cut two ½" x 12" (1.3 cm x 30.5 cm) strips. Arrange the framed photos, strips, and title box on the pages. Use adhesive to attach the components to the pages. Cut small sections from the paper doily. Place on the pages and press clear tiles over the top to secure.

MATERIALS

12" x 12" (30.5 cm x 30.5 cm) blue print paper

12" x 12" (30.5 cm x 30.5 cm) gray paper

paper in the following colors: dark gray, light gray, lavender, pink, blue polka dot

white tulle

clear plastic tiles

paper doily

blue embroidery floss

spray adhesive

double-sided adhesive sheet, such as Peel-N-Stick

TOOLS

metal-edged ruler

craft knife

scissors

tape

light blue paint with fine-tip applicator, such as Scribble Paint

wax paper

computer printer

Traveling, Summer 2004

gardens

down-town

hotel

Traveling

Punched paper and stamped fabric frames

Small accents can sometimes have a big pay-off. Add get-up-and-go to your travel photos with punched paper and stamped fabric corners.

Instructions for Assembling the Pages

1. With the ruler and knife, trim the unframed photos. Arrange and, with double-sided adhesive, attach them to the left-hand page. With the black ink, stamp the sun in the top right quadrant of the page. Let dry.

2. The frame is made for a 3½" x 4¾" (8.9 cm x 12.1 cm) photo. Make adjustments if your photo is a different size. From the gray paper, cut a 4" x 5¼" (10.2 cm x 13.3 cm) rectangle. Cut a 3" x 4¼" (7.6 cm x 10.8 cm) window in the center. Center and tape the photo to the back of the frame. Place the framed photo on the right-hand page and attach with double-sided adhesive. With scraps of paper, mask around the framed photo 1½" (3.8 cm) from the sides and 1¼" (3.1 cm) from the top and bottom. With the green ink, stamp the fern fronds in a random pattern. Let dry. Use the colored pencil to write a title and captions.

Instructions for the Punched Corners

1. Referring to the photo for colors, cut six 1½" (3.8 cm) squares. Punch a leaf in the center of three of the squares. Coat the backs of the punched squares with adhesive spray. Align the edges and press in place on the remaining squares. Use double-sided adhesive to attach to the corners of the photos.

Instructions for the Pillow Corners

1. Corners are made for 1½" x 1" (3.8 cm x 2.5 cm) rubber stamps. Make adjustments for stamps of different sizes. Cut 1½" x 1¼" (3.8 cm x 3.1 cm) rectangles at each corner. Cut four 2" (5.1 cm) squares from the fabric. With the brown ink, stamp the images in the centers of the fabric squares. Let dry.

2. Align the backing paper behind the page and draw a light line around the inside edge of each window. Attach a 2" (5.1 cm) square of double-sided adhesive sheet over each marked window. Remove the remaining protective paper to expose the adhesive. From the batting, cut four 1¼" x 1" (3.1 cm x 2.5 cm) rectangles. Center each inside the marked rectangles and attach to the adhesive. Center and place the stamped cloth rectangles on the batting and press the edges on the adhesive to secure.

3. Coat the back of the polka dot paper with spray adhesive. Press in place on the backing paper.

MATERIALS

12" x 12" (30.5 cm x 30.5 cm) gray paper

12" x 12" (30.5 cm x 30.5 cm) blue polka dot paper

12" x 12" (30.5 cm x 30.5 cm) backing paper

paper in the following colors: light green, sage green, yellow, dark gray

cream fabric

cotton quilt batting

spray adhesive

double-sided adhesive sheet, such as Peel-N Stick

TOOLS

metal-edged ruler

craft knife

pencil

scissors

rubber stamps with the following images: air mail medallion, suitcase, fern frond, sun

ink pads in the following colors: green, brown, black

oak leaf hole punch

maple leaf hole punch

brown colored pencil

Monochrome Kids

Fun folded paper corners

Nostalgic tokens of childhood, and snippets of folded paper, act as subtle but clever photo additions.

Instructions for Assembling the Pages

1. Trim the photos. Arrange the photos, postcard, Valentine, and wagon on the pages. Use adhesive to attach the components to the pages. Use the marker to write a title and caption.

Instructions for the Button Corner

1. Thread a short length of pearl cotton through the button holes. Knot and trim the thread ends. From the green paper, cut a ¾" (1.9 cm) square. Use double-sided adhesive to attach the button to the paper and to attach the paper to the photo corner.

Instructions for the Star Corner

1. From the vellum, cut a ½" x 4" (1.3 cm x 10.2 cm) strip. Referring to Diagram A (see below), fold at a right angle. Referring to Diagram B (see below), fold the ends to the center. Referring to Diagram C (see below), trim the ends. Place on the photo corner. Use the sharp point of the craft knife to pierce through the layered vellum and the page. Insert the star brad and secure through all layers.

Instructions for the Triangle Corners

1. From the red paper, cut a 1¼" (2 cm) square. Cut in half diagonally. From the vellum, cut two ½" x 3" (1.3 cm x 7.6 cm) strips. Referring to Diagram D (see below), fold the strips over the triangles. Referring to Diagram E (see below), trim the ends. Use adhesive to attach the triangles to the photo.

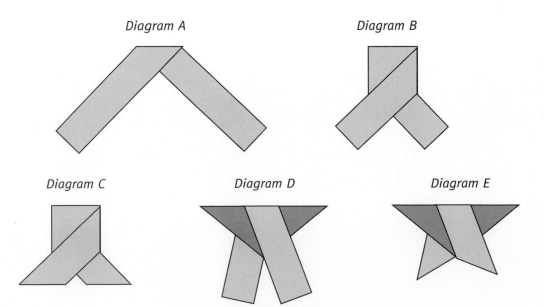

Diagram A   Diagram B

Diagram C   Diagram D   Diagram E

sight seeing

IMAGINE

- the aquatic Park
- the mosaic at Central Park
- up & down through the tree trunk
- exploring
- Climbing
- discovering

Imagine

Micro bead starburst corners

Capture the moment in time when it actually seems that time has stood still. Afternoons of exploration and discovery are defined with iridescent paper and bursts of micro beads.

Instructions for Assembling the Pages

1. From the silver film, cut four 5¾" (14.6 cm) squares. Coat the backs of the film with spray adhesive. Referring to the photo for placement, press in place on the right-hand page.

2. Trim the photos. Arrange the photos and the label on the pages. Use adhesive to attach them to the pages.

3. From the white paper, cut a 2" x 4½" (5.1 cm x 11.4 cm) rectangle. Coat the back of the rectangle with spray adhesive. Referring to the photo for placement, attach the rectangle to the right-hand page. From the white vellum, cut a 3¼" x 5" (8.2 cm x 12.7 cm) rectangle. Overhanging the bottom edge of the page, place the vellum rectangle over the white rectangle. Secure the vellum at the top corners with double-sided adhesive. Wrap the bottom edge to the back of the page and tape to secure. Use the marker to write captions.

Instructions for the Cosmic Corners

1. From the gold vellum, cut three 1¼" x 1½" (3.1 cm x 3.8 cm) rectangles. Coat the backs of the rectangles with spray adhesive. Press in place at the photo corners. Use the tracing paper to make the swirl templates (see below). Make two small swirls and one large swirl from double-sided adhesive. Peel the backing from the swirls, and overlapping the gold rectangles, attach them to the pages. Remove the remaining protective paper and sprinkle the beads on the exposed adhesive. Remove excess beads.

MATERIALS

12" x 12" (30.5 cm x 30.5 cm) gray paper

white paper

gold vellum

white vellum

faux metal label

silver micro beads

silver film

TOOLS

metal-edged ruler

craft knife

tracing paper

pencil

scissors

tape

black fine-tip marker

Small Swirl

Large Swirl

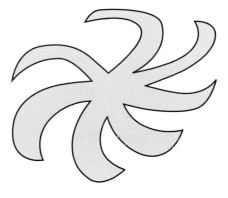

Our
Garden

Our Garden

Torn paper foliage corners

You don't need a green thumb to tear paper into vines and leaves. (Only opposing thumbs.) This foolproof treatment is great for beginners since you can't make a mistake when tearing.

MATERIALS

12" x 12"
(30.5 cm x 30.5 cm)
green paper

paper in the following colors: red gray/green, tan

spray adhesive

brown acrylic paint

TOOLS

metal-edged ruler

craft knife

tracing paper

pencil

scissors

paintbrush

Instructions for Assembling the Pages

1. Trim the photos and arrange them on the pages. Use adhesive to attach them to the pages. Paint the title on the page. Let dry.

Rose

Instructions for the Vine Corners

1. Tear strips from green paper. Fold to create contours. Tear leaves from green paper. Coat the backs of the leaves with spray adhesive. Press in place on the photo corners.

Instructions for the Rose Corners

1. Use the tracing paper to make the rose template (see above). From the red paper, cut two roses. From the tan paper, tear two 1½" (3.8 cm) wide ovals. From the green paper, tear six leaves. Coat the backs of the ovals, leaves, and roses with spray adhesive. Layer the elements in the same order and press in place at the corners.

Instructions for the Vine Corners

1. Tear strips from green paper. Fold to create contours. Tear leaves from green paper. Coat the backs of the vines and the leaves with spray adhesive. Press in place on the photo corners.

Babies

Diaper pin, teddy, and triangle corners

Nothing is cuter than a baby posing for a camera, but these corner accents come in a close second. You can coil, knot, and piece adorable corners for photos of diva babies.

Instructions for Assembling the Pages

1. Coat the backs of the pink print and pink stripe papers with spray adhesive. Referring to the photo, press in place on the pages. Trim the photos. Use the computer printer to print the title on the white paper. Coat the back of the tracing paper with spray adhesive. Press the tracing paper on the printed paper. Trim the title box through both layers.

2. Arrange the photos and title box on the pages. Use adhesive to attach the components to the pages. Use the marker to write captions.

Instructions for the Diaper Pin Corners

1. Use the tracing paper to make the diaper template (see page 90). From the white paper, cut four diaper corners. From the copper wire, cut two $4\frac{1}{2}$" (11.4 cm) lengths. With the pliers, shape the wire to match Diagram A (see page 90). Trim the wire ends. With the pliers, coil the chenille stems to match Diagram B (see page 90).

2. Attach narrow strips of the double-sided adhesive to the long sides of the diaper triangles. Overlapping at the centers, attach the triangles to the page corners. With the sharp point of the craft knife, pierce the top triangles at the marked points. Referring to the photo, insert the wire ends through the holes. Glue the coiled chenille over the wire ends with the hot glue gun.

Instructions for the Teddy Bear Corner

1. From the white paper, cut one $3\frac{1}{2}$" (8.9 cm) square. Use the tracing paper to make the templates (see page 90). Referring to the photo for colors, cut the shapes. Coat the backs of the shapes with spray adhesive. Referring to Assembled Bear Diagram (see page 90), place the shapes on the white paper in the following order: arms, body, head, snout, and foot pads. Press in place to adhere.

2. Trim the white paper to $2\frac{1}{2}$" x $2\frac{3}{4}$" (6.4 cm x 7 cm). Use the marker to draw the eyes, nose, and mouth where indicated. Use adhesive to attach the corner to the page.

Instructions for the Triangle Corners

1. From the polka dot paper, cut one $1\frac{1}{4}$" (3.1 cm) square. Cut in half diagonally. From the cord, cut two 3" (7.6 cm) lengths. Knot in the centers. Glue the knots to the triangles with the hot glue gun. Trim the cord ends. Attach the triangles at the photo corners with double-sided adhesive.

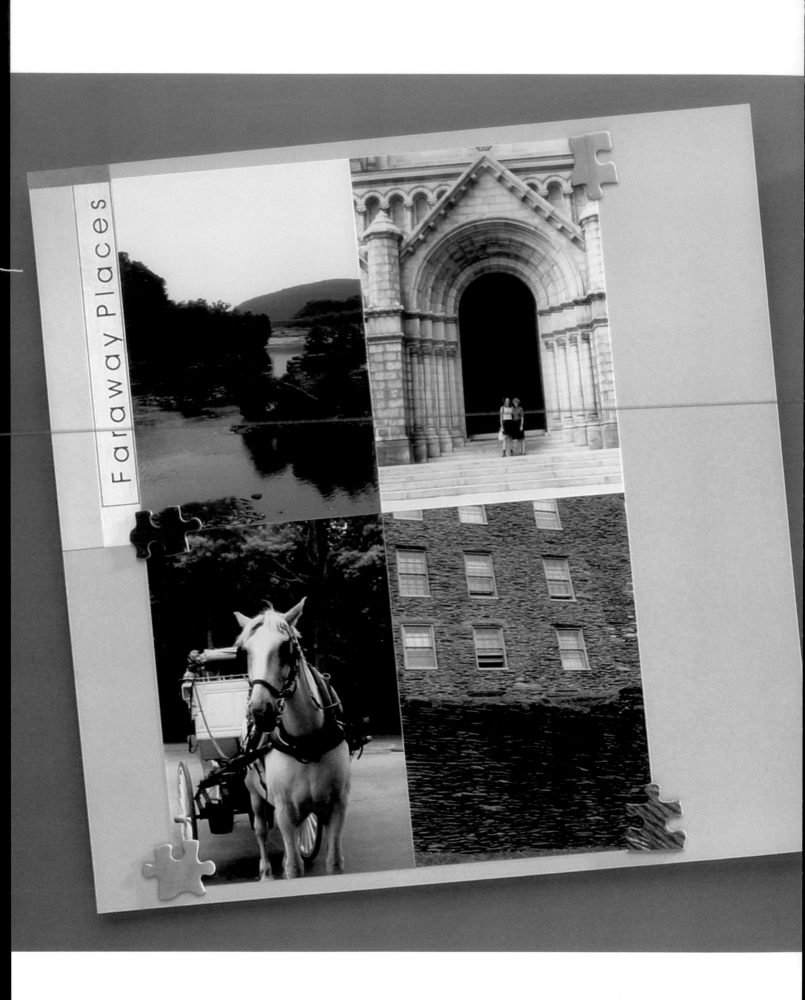

Faraway Places

Faraway Places

Puzzle piece corners

The original pixels: jigsaw puzzles pieces. Combine the pieces to create a graphic landscape and then break off the edges to accent your photos.

Instructions for Assembling the Pages

1. Use the computer printer to print the title on the white paper. (Make the type size ¾" [1.9 cm] tall.) Trim the title. From the lavender paper, cut one ¾" x 5¾" (1.9 cm x 14.6 cm) strip. From the purple paper, cut one ¼" x ½" (5 mm x 1.3 cm) strip. Coat the backs of the title box and paper strips with adhesive. Referring to the photo for placement, press in place at the corner of the left-hand page.

2. Trim the photos. Align the edge of the top photo with the title box and place the photos on the page. Use adhesive to attach the photos to the page.

3. Assemble the selected section of the jigsaw puzzle on a sheet of paper. Place a second sheet of paper over the top and turn the puzzle upside-down. Use the tracing paper to make a template that roughly matches the assembled pieces. Piecing if necessary, cut the shape from double-sided adhesive and attach it to the back of the puzzle. Attach the puzzle to the right-hand page. Attach selected loose puzzle pieces to the page.

Instructions for the Puzzle Corners

1. Attach selected loose puzzle pieces to the photo corners with double-sided adhesive.

MATERIALS

12" x 12" (30.5 cm x 30.5 cm) tan paper

paper in the following colors: white, lavender, purple

jigsaw puzzle

spray adhesive

double-sided adhesive sheet, such as Peel-N-Stick

TOOLS

metal-edged ruler

craft knife

computer printer

scissors

black fine-tip marker

Diagram A

TRIM

Diagram B

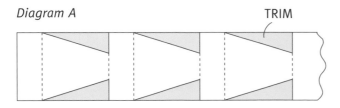

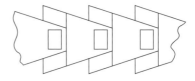

Having Fun

Pleated border and rainbow frames

What's black and white and hot all over? Black-and-white photos combined with glowing rainbow frames, of course. These eclectic outlines aren't confined to the edges of the photos. They zero in on the best parts of the images—the happy faces.

Instructions for the Pleated Border

1. From the cream print paper, cut two $1\frac{1}{2}$" x 12" (3.8 cm x 30.5 cm) strips. Referring to Diagram A (see opposite, below), fold the strips at $\frac{1}{2}$" (1.3 cm) and at $1\frac{1}{2}$" (3.8 cm) repeats. Cut triangles on both sides of the strips as indicated. Fold and trim the $\frac{1}{2}$" (1.3 cm)-wide sections to match the trimmed $1\frac{1}{2}$" (3.8 cm) sections. Place the folded strips, wrong-side-up, on the work surface. Cut short strips from double-sided adhesive. Referring to Diagram B (see opposite, below), attach them to the backs of the folded strips at the narrowest sections.

2. Starting in the top center of the page, overlap the narrow ends and attach the strips to the left-hand page. With the sharp point of the craft knife, pierce through the overlapping ends of the strips and through the page. Insert the silver brad and secure through all layers.

3. Use the tracing paper to make the Stem, Blossom, and Flower Center templates (see page 91). Referring to the photo for colors, cut four stems, blossoms, and centers. Slide the stems under the pleats. Coat the backs of the centers with spray adhesive and press in place on the blossoms. Coat the backs of the blossoms with spray adhesive and press in place on the tops of the stems. Attach the bottoms of the stems to the page with narrow strips of double-sided adhesive.

Instructions for the Rainbow Frames

1. Use the tracing paper to make the templates for the frames (see page 91). Enlarge or reduce if necessary to fit the selected photos. Referring to the photo for colors, cut one of each frame.

Instructions for Completing the Pages

1. Trim the background from the selected photo. Coat the back of the photo with spray adhesive. Mount the photo on the lavender paper. Trim the paper to a 7" x $5\frac{1}{2}$" (17.8 cm x 13.4 cm) rectangle. Coat the back of the rectangle with spray adhesive and mount the blue paper. Trim the blue paper to make a $\frac{1}{4}$" (5 mm) border. Stamp the title on the lavender paper. Let dry.

2. Trim the photos.

3. Arrange the mounted and unmounted photos on the pages. Use adhesive to attach the photos to the pages. Arrange the small frames on the photos. Coat the backs of the photos with spray adhesive and press in place to adhere.

MATERIALS

12" x 12" (30.5 cm x 30.5 cm) tangerine paper

12" x 12" (30.5 cm x 30.5 cm) orange paper

12" x 12" (30.5 cm x 30.5 cm) cream print paper

paper in the following colors: lavender, blue, light turquoise, dark turquoise, mint, periwinkle, pink, light green

silver brad

spray adhesive

double-sided adhesive sheet, such as Peel-N-Stick

TOOLS

metal-edged ruler

craft knife

tracing paper

scissors

pencil

alphabet rubber stamps

black ink pad

12" x 12"
(30.5 cm x 30.5 cm)
pink polka dot
paper

12" x 12"
(30.5 cm x 30.5 cm)
red paper

paper in the follow-
ing colors: light
green, Kelly green,
tan, cream, blue,
pink

alphabet stickers

round stickers

decorative paper
number

paper clips

spray adhesive

double-sided
adhesive sheet,
such as Peel-N-Stick

TOOLS

metal-edged ruler

craft knife

scissors

tape

black fine-tip
marker

Cherries Jubilee

Cherries border with paper clip and double frames

What do an ice cream sundae and a polka-dot page have in common? They are both topped with cherries. (In this case, rows and rows of cherries.) You could also use this border to color picnic or reunion pages.

Instructions for the Cherries Border

1. Use the tracing paper to make the templates (see opposite, below). From the red paper, cut two 12" (30.5 cm) long cherry strips. Referring to the diagram (see opposite, below), attach the wide bands of the strips to the pages with double-sided adhesive. From the light green paper, cut two ⅜" x 11" (1 cm x 27.9 cm) strips. Coat the backs of the strips with spray adhesive. Press in place on the red bands. Attach a small square of double-sided adhesive to the center of each cherry. Fold each cherry over the red/green band and attach each to the pages.

2. From the Kelly green paper, cut eighteen leaves. Coat the backs of the leaves with spray adhesive. Referring to the photo for placement, press in place on the red/green band. Attach round stickers to selected cherries.

Instructions for the Double Frames

1. The frame is made for a 5" x 6" (12.7 cm x 15.2 cm) photo. Make adjustments if your photo is a different size. From the blue paper, cut a 6¼" x 7¼" (15.8 cm x 18.4 cm) rectangle. Cut a 4½" x 5½" (11.4 cm x 13.4 cm) window in the center. From the tan paper, cut a 6¼" x 7¼" (15.8 cm x 18.4 cm) rectangle. Cut a 5" x 6" (12.7 cm x 15.2 cm) window in the center. Coat the back of the tan frame with spray adhesive. Center and press in place on the blue frame. Center and tape the photo to the back of the frame.

2. Repeat step 1 with blue and green papers. Center and tape the artwork to the back of the frame.

Instructions for the Paper Clip Frame

1. Trim the artwork to the desired size. Coat the back with spray adhesive. Mount the artwork on the pink paper. Trim the pink paper to make a narrow border. Slide the paper clips on the top edge.

Instructions for Completing the Pages

1. Attach the stickers to the light green paper for the title box. Use the marker to write a subtitle on the cream paper. Trim the green paper, cream paper, and decorative paper. Arrange the framed photo, framed artwork, mounted artwork, and title strips on the pages. Use adhesive to attach the components to the pages.

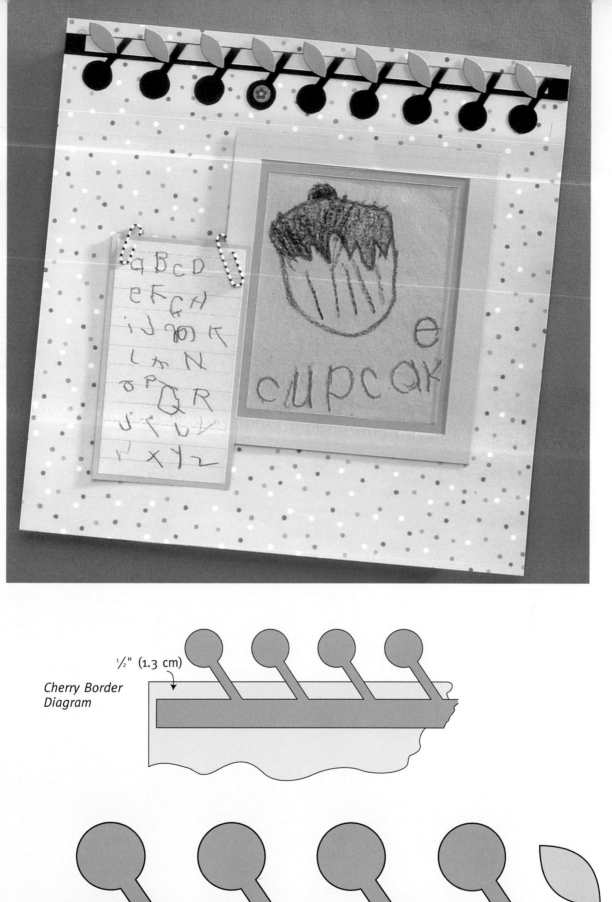

½" (1.3 cm)

*Cherry Border
Diagram*

*Cherry Border
Template*

Cami and Marissa at the airport

Summer 2004

saying
good-bye
to GERMANY

after traveling from Humboldt to
Frankfurt, we left Germany for
New York City. It was hard
saying good-bye to everyone,
but we looked forward to going
home to begin fall semester.

FROHSINN

Saying Good-Bye

Rustic wooden frame and corners

Handcrafted wooden corners and a carved timber frame add elegance to picturesque travel photos. After being charmed by the old-world details, it's hard saying good-bye.

Instructions for the Wooden Corners

1. Use the ruler and knife to cut two 1½" (3.8 cm) squares from the balsa wood. It will take several passes of the knife to cut completely through the wood. Cut both in half diagonally to make four triangles. Dilute the brown paint and paint the triangles. Let dry. Sand the edges and the tops to reveal the wood. Coat the backs of the tin corners with the craft glue and press in place on the wooden corners. Let dry.

2. Trim the photo. Use adhesive to mount the photo on the tan paper. Trim the paper to make narrow borders. Use double-sided adhesive to secure the corners to the photo.

Instructions for the Wooden Frame

1. The frame is made for a 5" x 3" (12.7 cm x 7.6 cm) photo. Make adjustments if your photo is a different size. With the ruler and knife, cut a 6" x 4" (15.2 cm x 10.2 cm) rectangle from the balsa wood. It will take several passes of the knife to cut completely through the wood. Cut a 4½" x 2½" (11.4 cm x 6.4 cm) window in the center.

2. Carefully cut small notches around the outside edges of the frame. Note that the wood breaks easily when working in the same direction as the wood grain. Use the sandpaper and the emery board to smooth the notched edges. Dilute the rust paint and paint the frame. Let dry. Center and tape the photo to the back of the frame.

3. From the dark gray paper, cut a 6¼" x 4¼" (15.8 cm x 10.8 cm) rectangle. With the sharp point of the craft knife, cut a small hole in the corners of the wooden frame and the paper. Insert the brads and secure through all layers.

Instructions for Completing the Pages

1. Coat the backs of the vellum sheet with spray adhesive. Align the outside edges and press in place on the tan paper. Trim the remaining photos.

2. Use the computer printer to print the title and a caption on the taupe print paper. Trim or tear the title and caption boxes. Arrange the unframed photos, framed photo, mounted photo, hinges, title box, and caption box. Use adhesive to attach the components to the pages.

3. Attach the sticker. Use the sharp point of the craft knife to pierce the caption box and the page. Pierce the sticker and the page. Insert brads and secure through all layers. Use the marker to write messages.

MATERIALS

12" x 12" (30.5 cm x 30.5 cm) tan paper

12" x 12" (30.5 cm x 30.5 cm) printed vellum

paper in the following colors: tan, gray, taupe print

balsa wood

silver brads

sticker

tin filigree corners

silver hinges

brown acrylic paint

rust acrylic paint

spray adhesive

double-sided adhesive sheet, such as Peel-N-Stick

TOOLS

metal-edged ruler

craft knife

emery board

fine sandpaper

craft glue

tape

computer printer

black fine-tip marker

Doorways

Bower borders and photo toppers

The symbol of the doorway is one of the most intriguing and endearing in all of art, literature, and mythology. Who can resist wondering what waits on the other side? Especially behind such welcoming doorways as these.

Instructions for Assembling the Pages

1. With the ruler and knife, trim the photos.

2. Use adhesive to mount the selected photos on the gray and pink papers. Trim the colored papers to make narrow borders. Note that the large photo has a border on only the top and sides.

3. From the lavender paper, cut a 1¼" x 12" (3.1 cm x 30.5 cm) strip. Use the computer printer to print captions on the white paper. Trim the captions. Apply a light coat of chalk to the caption boxes and rub with a tissue to distribute the color.

4. Arrange the mounted photos, unmounted photo, lavender strip, and caption boxes on the pages. Use adhesive to attach the components to the pages.

Instructions for Bower Border

1. Use the tracing paper to make the sleeve template (see opposite, below). From the gold paper, cut one sleeve. Fold where indicated. Attach one small strip of double-sided adhesive to the back of the sleeve. Center and press in place on the top of the page.

2. With the wire cutters, cut four 7" (17.8 cm) lengths of stems. Overlapping the ends at the center, arrange on the open sleeve. With small stitches spaced approximately ½" (1.3 cm) apart, stitch the stems to the page to secure. Tape the thread ends to the back of the page.

3. Fold the sleeve ends in and use a small square of double-sided adhesive to secure the ends together. Apply a small drop of craft glue to the back of the angel charm and attach it to the sleeve. Let dry.

Instructions for Bower Toppers

1. Cut one 5½" (13.4 cm) stem and two 7" (17.8 cm) stems. Place the short stem horizontally on the work surface. Referring to Diagram A (right), place the long stems perpendicular on the short stem, 1¼" (3.1 cm) from the left end. Use the embroidery floss to lash the stems together at the intersection. Knot the floss and trim the floss ends.

2. Referring to Diagram B (opposite, right), bend the long stems together and lash the ends together at the opposite end of the short stem. Knot the floss and trim the floss ends. Attach double-sided adhesive to the back of the green paper scraps. Cut into narrow strips. Remove remaining protective paper and place the strips over stems at selected points to secure to the page.

3. Repeat steps 1 and 2 to make second Bower Topper.

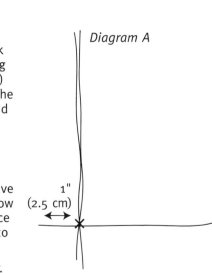

Diagram A

1"
(2.5 cm)

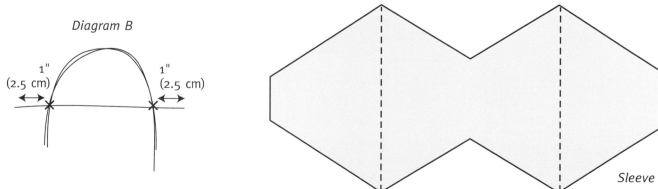

Diagram B

1"
(2.5 cm)

1"
(2.5 cm)

Sleeve

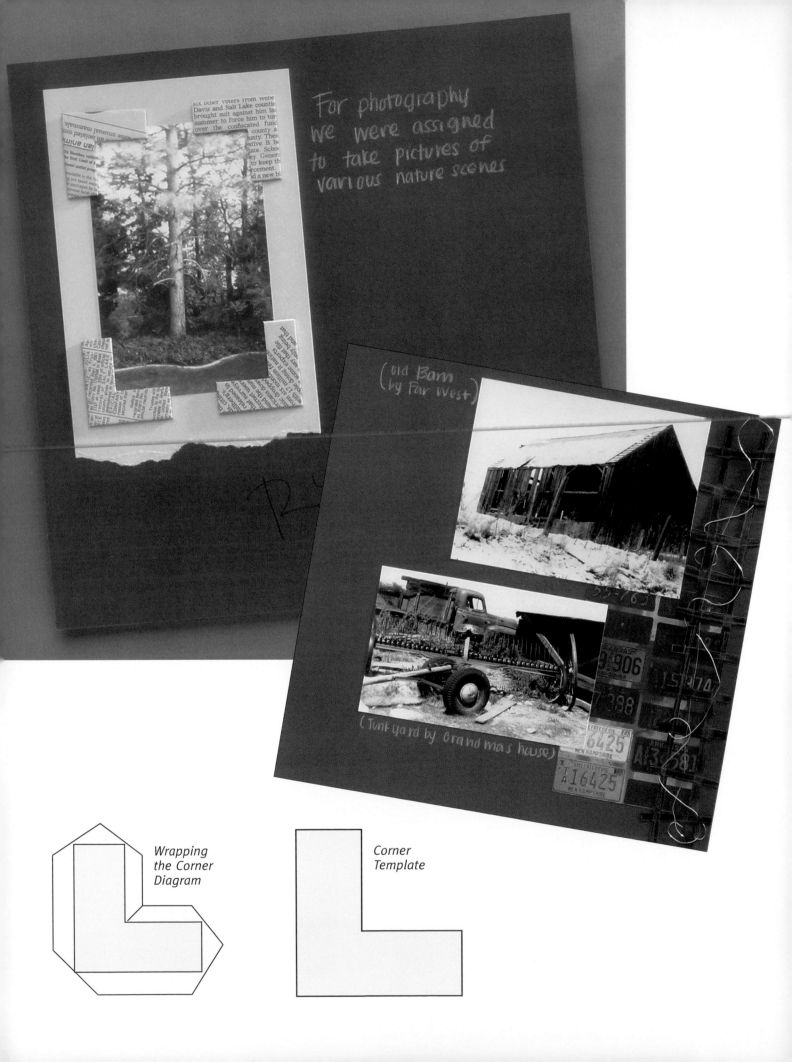

For photography
we were assigned
to take pictures of
various nature scenes

(old Barn
by Far West)

(Junkyard by Grandma's house)

Wrapping the Corner Diagram

Corner Template

Rust and Splinters

Newsprint corners and railroad track border

A lazy afternoon that included a new roll of film and a full tank of gas produced a synthesis of aging textures and surfaces. Decorate studies of ordinary objects with ordinary accents that include old newspapers and silver wire.

MATERIALS

12" 12"
(30.5 cm x 30.5 cm)
brown paper

gray paper

black paper

newspaper

decorative paper

silver 32 mm
gauge wire

balsa wood

spray adhesive

double-sided
adhesive sheet,
such as Peel-N-Stick

TOOLS

metal-edged ruler

craft knife

tracing paper

pencil

scissors

wire cutters

colored pencils in
the following colors:
black, white, tan

Instructions for the Print-Covered Corners

1. Use the tracing paper to make the templates (see opposite, below right). Use the ruler and knife to cut four corners from the balsa wood. It will take several passes of the knife to cut completely through the wood. Note that the wood breaks easily when working in the same direction as the wood grain.

2. Referring to the diagram (see opposite, below left), cut a piece from the newspaper. Coat the back of the newspaper with spray adhesive. Wrap the newspaper around the corner piece. Repeat with the remaining corners.

3. Trim the photo. Use adhesive to mount the photo on the gray paper. Trim the top and sides of the gray paper to make ¾" (1.9 cm) borders. Tear the bottom edge of the gray paper. Use double-sided adhesive to secure the corners to the photo.

Instructions for the Railroad Tracks Border

1. From the black paper, cut two 6" (15.2 cm) lengths of railroad tracks. Draw irregular outlines on the tracks with the white colored pencil. Coat the backs of the tracks with spray adhesive. Overlapping the ends slightly, place the tracks on the work surface. Cut a 45" (114.3 cm) length of silver wire and weave the wire around and through the tracks in a freeform pattern. Coil the wire ends in at the bottom of the tracks.

Instructions for Completing the Pages

1. Trim the remaining photos and decorative paper. Arrange the mounted photo, unmounted photos, and decorative paper on the pages. Use adhesive to secure the components to the pages. Press the tracks along the edge of the paper. Use the black colored pencil to write the title and the tan pencil to write the captions.

Railroad Tracks

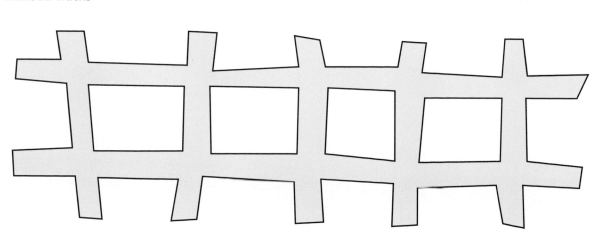

Reflections

Lisa

High School Grad

College
Graduation
1980

Reflections

Jeweled corner and serpentine border

Foggy images, tender feelings, beckoning sounds, and flowery smells are important memory snippets that describe who we are. Make a paper and photo collage to chronicle your past and to provoke personal ephemera.

Instructions for Assembling the Pages

1. Cut a 6" x 8" (15.2 cm x 20.3 cm) rectangle from the dictionary and toile papers. From the olive polka dot paper, cut one 8½" x 12" (21.6 cm x 30.5 cm) rectangle. Trim the photos.

2. Stamp a rose on one large tag. Let dry. Shade the rose with the colored pencils. Cut small scraps from the decorative papers. Coat the backs of the scraps with spray adhesive and attach them to the medium tag and the remaining large tag. From the rayon trim, cut three 4" (10.2 cm) lengths. Thread the lengths through the tags and knot.

3. Trim the photos. Arrange the photos, polka dot paper, dictionary paper, toile paper, and tags on the pages. Use adhesive to attach the components to the pages.

4. Stamp the pears on the tops of the pages. Let dry. Shade the pears with the colored pencils. From the green vellum, tear a 2½" x 6½" (6.4 cm x 16.5 cm) rectangle. Coat the back of the rectangle with spray adhesive and press in place over the two stamped pears. Tear a 3" x 3" (7.6 cm x 7.6 cm) square. Coat with spray adhesive and press in place over the single stamped pear.

Instructions for the Jeweled Corner

1. Cut a 1" (2.5 cm) square from the fabric. Remove a few loose threads along the cut edges to fray slightly. Press the prongs of the jewel stud through the fabric scrap. Place the jewel on the photo corner and mark the insertion points for the prongs. With the sharp point of the craft knife, pierce the fabric at the marked points. Insert the prongs through all layers and bend them flat with the spoon or knife.

Instructions for the Serpentine Border

1. Cut one yard (0.9 m) of rayon trim. Overhang the top edge of the page with the looped end, and place the trim on the paper. Shape the trim into freeform lines of bends and curls. Place the jewels over the trim, and mark the insertion points for the prongs. With the sharp point of the craft knife, pierce the paper at the marked points. Insert the prongs through all layers and bend them flat with the spoon or knife. Tape the top loop of the trim to the back of the page. Trim the ends.

MATERIALS

12" x 12" (30.5 cm x 30.5 cm) cream paper

12" x 12" (30.5 cm x 30.5 cm) olive polka dot paper

dictionary print paper

lavender toile paper

turquoise vellum

decorative papers

1¼ yards (1.1 m) tufted rayon trim

square jewel studs

two large paper tags

one medium paper tag

scrap pink moiré fabric

spray adhesive

double-sided adhesive sheet, such as Peel-N-Stick

TOOLS

metal-edged ruler

craft knife

scissors

tape

rose rubber stamp

pear rubber stamp

brown ink pad

colored pencils

blunt tool (spoon or knife)

black fine-tip marker

12" x 12"
(30.5 cm x 30.5 cm)
lined composition
paper

12" x 12"
(30.5 cm x 30.5 cm)
gold print paper

preprinted title

paper in the follow-
ing colors: tan, gray,
mauve, red, green

paper clips

photo of stairs

small notebook
with spiral binding

air-drying
modeling clay,
such as PaperClay

acrylic paint in the
following colors:
gold, orange, white,
black

stickers

alphabet paper

spray adhesive

double-sided
adhesive sheet,
such as Peel-N-Stick

craft glue

TOOLS

metal-edged ruler

craft knife

tracing paper

pencil

tape

scissors

paintbrush

sandpaper

colored pencils

black fine-tip marker

Back to School

School-themed frames and apple corner

School photos—they go from the classroom to the refrigerator door to the junk drawer to the shoe box. Rescue your favorites and choose these elementary techniques to make display frames. Then, they can go straight to your album.

Instructions for the Paper Clip Frame

1. The frame is made for a 3¼" x 4½" (8.2 cm x 11.4 cm) photo. Make adjustments if your photo is a different size. From the tan paper, cut a 4" x 6" (10.2 x 15.2 cm) rectangle. Cut an off-kilter 2¾" x 4" (7 cm x 10.2 cm) window. Center and tape the photo to the back of the frame. Slide the paper clips on the side of the frame.

Instructions for the Doorway Frame

1. The frame is made for a 2½" x 3¾" (6.4 cm x 9.5 cm) photo. Make adjustments if your photo is a different size. From the gray paper, cut a 2¾" x 4¾" (7 cm x 12.1 cm) rectangle. Leaving 1¼" (3.1 cm) on the bottom of the frame, cut a 2" x 3¼" (5.1 cm x 8.2 cm) window. Use the colored pencils to draw a recessed panel and a doorknob on the frame. Center and tape the photo to the back of the frame.

Instructions for the Notebook Frame

1. The frame is made for a 2½" x 3½" (6.4 cm x 8.9 cm) photo. Make adjustments if your photo is a different size. Cut a 2" x 3" (5.1 cm x 7.6 cm) window in the cover of the notebook. Center and tape the photo to the back of the cover. Place the notebook on the work surface and flatten the wire coils.

Instructions for the Pencil Frame

1. The frame is made for a 3¼" x 4¼" (8.2 cm x 10.8 cm) photo. Make adjustments if your photo is a different size. From the clay, shape a ⅜" x 3" (1 cm x 7.6 cm) tube. Let dry. Trim the ends. Shave one end to resemble a pencil point. Flatten a long flat side by sanding down with sandpaper. Paint with the acrylic paints: Use gold paint for the shaft, orange for the eraser, white for the point, and black for the tip. Let dry.

2. From the mauve paper, cut a 4" x 5" (10.2 cm x 12.7 cm) rectangle. Center and cut a 2¾" x 3¾" (7 cm x 9.5 cm) window. Center and tape the photo to the back of the frame. Use the craft glue to glue the pencil to the top of the frame. Let dry.

Instructions for the Apple Corner

1. Use the tracing paper to make the templates (see opposite). From the red paper, cut an apple. From the green paper, cut a stem/leaf.

Instructions for Completing Pages

1. Trim the title box. Cut out the selected paper letters. Cut the stairs from the stairs photo. From the gold print paper, cut a 2½" x 12" (6.4 cm x 30.5 cm) strip. Tear one long side of the strip. Arrange the torn strip, framed photos, unframed photo, title box, and stairs on the pages. Use adhesive to attach the components to the pages. Attach the stickers to the pages. Use the marker to write captions.

Back to School

Stem/Leaf

Apple

12" x12"
(30.5 cm x 30.5 cm)
black paper

12" x 12"
(30.5 cm x 30.5 cm)
gray paper

paper in the follow-
ing colors: red,
white, tan, pink,
lavender

pink striped vellum

spray adhesive

double-sided
adhesive sheet,
such as Peel-N-Stick

TOOLS

metal-edged ruler

craft knife

hot glue gun

tape

tracing paper

pencil

scissors

pink colored pencil

black colored pencil

The Adventures of Super Dog

Book border and bed frame

It isn't just kids who dream of growing up to become superheroes. Immortalize your mild-mannered underdog with a special story and a visual tribute. You may not get applause, but you will get a nice, wet kiss.

Instructions for the Book Border

1. From the white paper, cut two $3\frac{1}{4}$" x $1\frac{1}{2}$" (8.2 cm x 3.8 cm) rectangles. From the red paper, cut two $3\frac{1}{4}$" x $1\frac{3}{4}$" (8.2 cm x 4.4 cm) rectangles. Fold the white rectangles in half. Attach narrow strips of double-sided adhesive to the short sides. Apply a thin line of glue to the folded edges with the glue gun. Press in place in the centers of the red rectangles. Let dry. Remove the remaining protective paper from the adhesive strips and, with the paper slightly bowed, attach the sides to the red rectangles.

2. From the vellum, cut two $\frac{1}{4}$" x $3\frac{1}{4}$" (5 mm x 8.2 cm) strips. Tape the ends to the back of the books. Fold over the tops of the books and crease the strips. Attach small squares of double-sided adhesive to the ends of the strips.

3. From the vellum, cut two $3\frac{3}{4}$" x 12" (9.5 cm x 30.5 cm) strips. Coat the backs of the strips with spray adhesive. Press in place along the tops of the pages. Coat the backs of the books with spray adhesive. Press in place at the top corners of the pages. Remove the remaining protective paper from the adhesive squares and, with the bookmarks slightly bowed, attach them to the pages.

Instructions for the Bed Frame

1. Use the tracing paper to make the templates (see page 92). Referring to the photo for colors, cut one of each shape.

2. Arrange the shapes on the right-hand page. Coat the backs of the shapes with spray adhesive. Noting overlaps, press in place on the page.

Instructions for Completing the Pages

1. With the ruler and knife, trim the photos. Cut the artwork into a cloud shape. Cut two small cloud shapes from the white paper. Assemble the photos, artwork, and small clouds on the pages. Use adhesive to attach the components to the pages. Use the pink colored pencil to write a story. Use the black colored pencil to write a caption.

(Cookie with dreams of Granduer.)

Once upon a time there lived a mild-manored dog named cookie. She looked normal enough at a glance.....

But when called into action she became Super Dog. When she put on her cape she had the strength of ten dogs. On one such occassion, July 12, mysterious happened

happy birthday!

Party Guests:
Brianne
Liza
Beck
Spencer
Mackay
Angela
Tracee
Blair
Annabelle
Lake

Birthday Cake

Candle frames and cake slice border

Question: Who has more fun—the birthday kid, the party guests, or the photographer? Answer: None of the above. You will have the most fun of all making these paper pieced party pages.

Instructions for the Candle Frames

1. The large frame is made for a 5" x 3¼" (12.7 cm x 8.2 cm) photo. Make adjustments if your photo is a different size. From the polka-dot paper, cut one 6¼" x 4½" (15.8 cm x 11.4 cm) rectangle. Center and cut a 4½" x 2¾" (11.4 cm x 7 cm) frame. Center and tape the photo to the back of the frame.

2. Cut three 1" (2.5 cm) lengths of pearl cotton. Place them on the frame. From the green paper, cut three ¼" (5 mm) strips of various lengths. Covering the bottoms of the wicks, attach the candles to the frame with double-sided adhesive.

3. The small frame is made for a 2½" x 3" (6.4 cm x 7.6 cm) photo. Making adjustments for the smaller size, repeat steps 1 and 2 to complete the frame.

Instructions for the Cake Border

1. Use the tracing paper to make the templates (see page 93). Referring to the photo for colors, cut out four frosting shapes, four cake-top shapes, eight layer shapes, and three forks. From the purple paper, cut two ¾" x 12" (1.9 cm x 30.5 cm) strips. Cut shallow scallops along one side of the strips.

2. Trim the photos. Slide the photos between the fork tines. Noting overlaps, arrange the scallops, forks, and cake shapes on the pages. Note that the layers overlap the cake-top shapes. Coat the backs of the shapes with spray adhesive and press in place on the pages. Cut four 1" (2.5 cm) lengths of pearl cotton. Place them on the cake slices. From the green paper, cut four ¼" x 1" (5 mm x 2.5 cm) strips. Covering the bottoms of the wicks, attach the candles to the cake slices with the double-sided adhesive.

Instructions for Completing the Pages

1. Use the computer printer to print a caption on the lavender paper. Trim the caption box to an irregular shape. Coat the back of the caption box with spray adhesive and press in place on the page. Use the yellow chalk to write a title.

MATERIALS

12" x 12" (30.5 cm x 30.5 cm) brown paper

paper in the following colors: turquoise, gold, lavender, green, gray, purple, blue polka dot

cream pearl cotton

spray adhesive

double-sided adhesive sheet, such as Peel-N-Stick

TOOLS

metal-edged ruler

craft knife

tracing paper

pencil

tape

scissors

computer printer

yellow chalk

SPORTS BRIEFS

homes will eventually fill a 6.5-acre parcel in an area originally intended for less dense housing, although the rezone approval by the Hooper City Council raised the question of when development will slow in the small rural community.

"Look at all the building that's going on out here right now. We have more than 900 homes on the books, our plate's pretty full. ... We don't need any more building right now," said Councilman Richard Noyes.

Nonetheless, the small acreage owned by Ralph Miles at 4924 W. 5500 South was rezoned by a vote of four to two.

The development, which was originally zoned for one-acre lots, will be comprised of properties that can accommodate smaller homes on lots of a minimum of 13,000 square feet.

According to City Engineer Tracy Allen, the property in question suits the city's master plan for smaller lots. He also said collateral factors such as its proximity to the Legacy Highway and adjacent higher-density developments make it a good fit for a rezoning action.

Resident Shawn Beus agreed. "I hope you will consider the effectiveness of the land. The useage as a residential setting is in the property owners' best interest and fits the overall community plan. Please consider (the proposal to rezone) independently of other large developments," he said.

Mayor Glenn Barrow said he was intrigued by developer Miles' ideas of building some housing for seniors that would have handicapped access and other features such as one-story construction.

"There's a huge question mark about how all this is going to play out. We do have 900 homes approved ... We're on a train and we don't know when it will stop," added Councilman Theo Cox.

Lyle Taylor, newly elected to the council, made it clear that his constituents desire no further action on approving more dense developments and, along with Noyes, voted against the rezoning action.

continue to wring our chubby little hands over how to fix this obesity epidemic. The answer seems obvious, yet few of us have the will power to put down that drumstick and pick up that dumbbell.

But Dave Greiling has an idea.

Dave is an editor here at the Standard-Examiner. As any writer can tell you, editors rarely have ideas — let alone good ones — so when they do actually hit upon something like this, it's vitally important to reward that initiative by mocking it in print.

His suggestion? A fat tax.

No, not a "flat" tax, but an actual "fat" tax. Make Americans pay their taxes by the pound. For example, you take the combined total weight of a taxpayer and his or her dependents and divide that number by their combined height. Then, using a complicated IRS formula that, frankly, you just wouldn't understand (multiply by 10), we arrive at a tax-burden percentage.

For example, consider a family of four with an annual income of $80,000. If their combined height is 18 feet 4 inches, and together they weigh a slightly portly 783 pounds, they'll pay $28,473 in taxes. But if each family member lost just 10 pounds, the resulting tax break would save them nearly $1,500 annually. And imagine if they lost some serious weight, like one of them developed an eating disorder or got sick or something.

But the best part of all this would be that the weeks leading up to an April 15 weigh-in become a festive time of anticipation, with the entire country resembling a high school ... to make weight ... abusing diuretics and ... cups all day. Good,

g earns praise

The findings were published in Thursday's New England Journal of Medicine. The research was partly funded by Pfizer Inc., the maker of Aromasin.

Dr. Jeff Abrams, the National Cancer Institute's associate chief of clinical research, said a recent study on exemestane "cousin" letrozole showed important advantages over tamoxifen for the class.

"I think with these two studies together, the strategy of switching from tamoxifen to these aromatase inhibitors will become a new standard," said Abrams, who was not involved in the study.

Several recent studies have shown that exemestane and other aromatase inhibitors also work longer, with less toxicity, than tamoxifen in women whose breast cancer had spread to other areas. Exemestane also has been shown to prolong the survival of women with advanced breast cancer after tamoxifen and other drugs fail.

"This whole class of drugs looks very promising, very active," said Dr. Julia Smith, clinical associate professor of oncology at the NYU medical school and cancer institute.

The study, which involved 4,742 postmenopausal women in 37 countries, focused on women with breast cancer in which the hormone estrogen fuels tumor growth — the type responsible for about 70 percent of breast cancer.

Tamoxifen, the celebrated drug credited with slashing breast cancer death rates worldwide, could be eclipsed by a newer medicine that is even more effective at preventing recurrence of the disease in women whose tumors were caught early and removed.

A large, international study of postmenopausal women with early-stage cancer found that those who took tamoxifen for 2½ years and then switched to exemestane for another 2½ years were one-third less likely to suffer a recurrence than those who took tamoxifen the whole time.

The women switching to exemestane also had less-serious side effects, were 56 percent less likely to get cancer in the other breast and were half as likely to develop unrelated cancer in other parts of the body.

Lead researcher Dr. R.C. Coombes, professor of cancer medicine at Imperial College School of Medicine in London, predicted doctors will give exemestane to many women at high risk for recurrence, such as those whose breast cancer has spread to multiple lymph nodes.

Exemestane, which went on the market for advanced breast cancer, is a hormonal ... the brand Aromasin. It i... breast cancer drug...

LOCAL GIRL MAKES GOOD

seconds on the shot clock," Drisdom said of Woodberry's critical foul. "He was pressuring me, and I had no choice but to try to drive on him. He didn't want me to ... by him, so he had to reach out. I started to get by him and he lunged at me a little bit and lost his balance.

"It was so ridiculous. I would kick myself if I ... him."

"The fact that we g... a new clock (thanks t... Woodberry's untimel... foul), it really was b... us," said Utah senio... Nick Jacobson, wh... a game-high 19 po... "With the things t...

Coverings - Home Depot
Demonstration - Home Depot, Ogden
Home Interiors & Gifts - Lisa Anderson
Gerry Richards, Team One at Coldwell Banker Residential Brokerage
stand of eco-system maintenance & filtration, Jeff Booth, Tesch Landscaping

stand of eco-system maintenance & filtration, Jeff Booth, Tesch Landscaping
Demonstration - Home Depot, Ogden
Fallon, ASID, CKD, Instile & Rail
Gerry Richards, Team One at Coldwell Banker Residential Brokerage
Birds And Blooms - Bill Fenimore, Wild Bird Center
Coverings - Home Depot
Home Depot, Ogden
Home Interiors & Gifts - Lisa Anderson
Gerry Richards, Team One at Coldwell Banker Residential Brokerage
Wahlstrom, director

Home Depot, Ogden
Birds And Blooms - Bill Fenimore, Wild Bird Center
Richards, Team One at Coldwell Banker Residential Brokerage
Demonstration - Home Depot, Ogden
Coverings - Home Depot
Gerry Richards, Team One at Coldwell Banker Residential Brokerage

"That's why I do what I do."

First Place

Local Girl Makes Good

Newsprint frame and soccer ball border

Stop the presses! You can scoop your local sports writer with the release of these sensational pages. With this kind of encouragement, it won't be long before your budding athlete is featured in the real thing.

Instructions for the Newspaper Frame

1. The frame is made for a 4" x 5½" (10.2 cm x 13.4 cm) photo. Make adjustments if your photo is a different size. Make a black-and-white copy of your photo with the copy machine. Lightly shade the photo with the colored pencils. In the top left quadrant of the left-hand page, cut a 3½" x 5" (8.9 cm x 12.7 cm) window. Center and tape the photo to the back of the page.

2. Use the computer printer to print the title on the white paper. Trim the title box. Cut sections from the newspaper and piece them together to cover the page. Coat the backs of the title box and newspaper sections with spray adhesive. Press in place to adhere.

Instructions for the Soccer Border

1. From the olive polka dot paper, cut a 1¾" x 12" (4.4 cm x 30.5 cm) strip. Cut an irregular edge along one side. From the white paper, cut two 1¾" (4.4 cm)-wide circles, and two 1⅝" (4.1 cm)-wide circles. From the tan paper, cut one 1¾" (4.4 cm)-wide circle. From the black and the brown papers, cut confetti shapes, measuring between ¼" and ⅜" (5 mm and 1 cm) square. Noting overlaps, arrange the strip, circles, and confetti on the right hand page. Coat the backs with spray adhesive and press in place along the edge of the page.

Instructions for Completing the Pages

1. Trim the photos. From the taupe print paper, cut one 4" x 6" (10.2 cm x 15.2 cm) rectangle. From the blue paper, tear a blue ribbon. Trim the message box into an irregular shape.

2. Noting overlaps, arrange the photos, paper rectangle, blue ribbon, message box, and remaining confetti on the page. Use adhesive to attach the components to the page. Use the black colored pencil to decorate the ribbon.

MATERIALS

12" x 12" (30.5 cm x 30.5 cm) tan paper

12" x 12" (30.5 cm x 30.5 cm) olive polka-dot paper

newspapers

paper in the following colors: black, white, tan, brown, blue, taupe print

preprinted message

spray adhesive

double-sided adhesive sheet, such as Peel-N-Stick

TOOLS

metal edged ruler

craft knife

scissors

tape

copy machine

computer printer

black colored pencil

Templates and Diagrams

Sepia Dancers, page 27

Pool Party, page 29

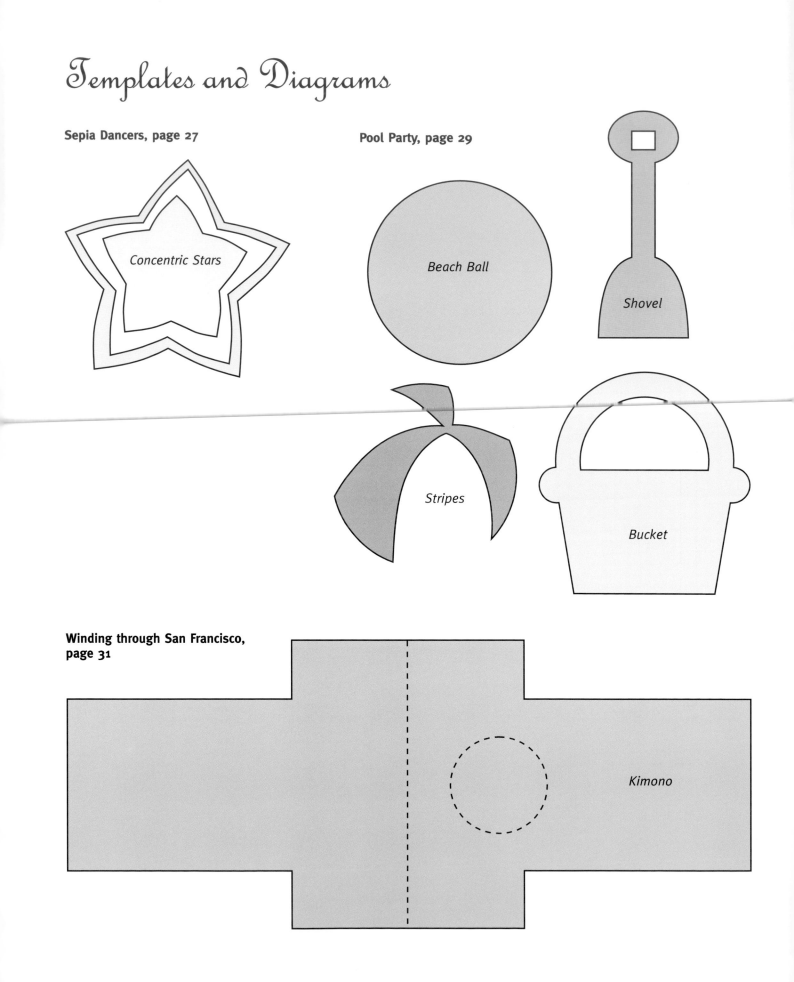

Concentric Stars

Beach Ball

Shovel

Stripes

Bucket

Winding through San Francisco, page 31

Kimono

Ionic column

Concentric pediments

Four-Leaf Clover

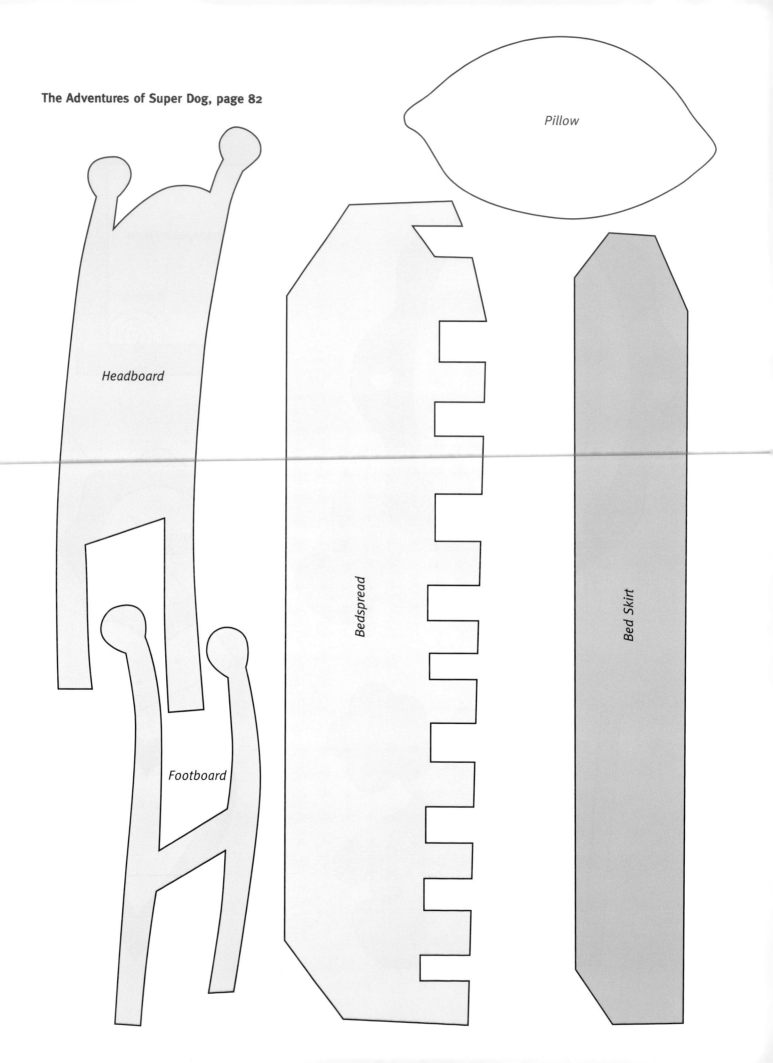

Pillow

Headboard

Footboard

Bedspread

Bed Skirt

Birthday Cake, page 85

Frosting

Cake Top

Layer

Fork

Resources

3M
www.mmm.com
spray adhesive, laminating sheets

Artistic Wire
www.artisticwire.com
wire

Aussie Scrapbook Suppliers
www.scrapbooking.about.com
supplies

Berwick Offray LLC
www.berwickindustries.com
ribbon

Canadian Scrapbook Stores
www.welovescrapbooking.com/stores
supplies

Canson
www.canson-us.com
paper

Clearsnap, Inc.
www.clearsnap.com
ink pads

Craf-T Products
www.craf-tproducts.com
decorative chalk

Creative Paperclay
www.paperclay.com
air-drying modeling clay

DMC
www.dmc-usa.com
pearl cotton

DMD Industries
www.dmdind.com
decorative paper

Daisy D's Paper
www.daisydspaper.com
paper

Darice
www.darice.com
tin snowflakes

Deluxe Cuts
www.deluxecuts.com
die-cut shapes

Die Cuts With a View
www.diecutswithaview.com
faux metallic letters

Duncan Enterprises
www.duncancrafts.com
3-D paint

EK Success
www.eksuccess.com
pens and markers

Emagination Crafts, Inc.
www.emaginationcrafts.com
paper punches

FoofaLa
www.foofala.com
hinges, decorative papers

Franca Xenia
www.paperworld.co.za
supplies

Glitterex Corp.
Cranford, NJ 07016
(908) 272-9121
glitter

The Gold Leaf Company
www.goldleafcompany.com
composition gold leaf

Halcraft
www.halcraft.com
beads

Hallmark
www.hallmark.com
stickers

Hero Arts
www.heroarts.com
rubber stamps

Hirschberg Schutz & Co.
Union, New Jersey 07083
(908) 810-1111
decorative rhinestones

Hunt Corporation
www.hunt-corp.com
craft knife

International Scrapbook stores
www.memorymakers.com
/locator/store
supplies

JHB International
www.buttons.com
buttons

Karen Foster Design
www.karenfosterdesign.com
paper

Magic Mesh
www.magicmesh.com
adhesive mesh

Making Memories
www.makingmemories.com
plastic disks

Mead Corporation
www.meadweb.com
notebook

Memory Lane
www.memorylanepaper.com
paper, eyelets

PSX
www.psxdesign.com
rubber stamps

Pebbles Inc.
www.pebblesinc.com
paper

Personal Impressions
www.richstamp.co.uk
supplies

Plaid Enterprises
www.plaidonline.com
acrylic paint, silk ribbon

Ranger Industries
www.rangerink.com
ink pads

Rubber Stampede, Inc.
www.rubberstampede.com
rubber stamps

SEI
www.shopsei.com
paper

Sanford Corporation
www.sanfordcorp.com
colored pencils

Stampendous
www.stampendous.com
embossing powder

Stamperia
www.stamperia.com
supplies

Sticker Studio
www.stickerstudio.com
stickers

Therm O Web
www.thermoweb.com
double-sided adhesive

Westrim
www.westrimcrafts.com
wire

About the Author

Trice Boerens has worked in the paper and craft industry for 23 years as a product designer, art director, and author. She has designed craft projects for kits and books and has also designed consumer goods that include wallpaper, linens, and jewelry. She is a graduate of Brigham Young University with a degree in art education and graphic design.

Acknowledgments

Thank you to Mary Ann Hall, Lisa Chandler, and Kevin Dilley.